Managing Licensed
E-Resources

Managing Licensed E-Resources

Techniques, Tips, and Practical Advice

*by 11 past and present managers of e-resource
collections and e-resource licensing experts*

Galadriel Chilton (Editor), Stephanie Willen Brown, Anna
Creech, Lindsay Cronk, Joan M. Emmet, Scarlet Galvan,
Athena Hoeppner, Jenifer S. Holman, Erika Ripley, Allyson
Rodriguez, and Angela Sidman

PACIFIC
UNIVERSITY
PRESS

FOREST GROVE, OREGON

PACIFIC UNIVERSITY PRESS
2043 College Way
Forest Grove, Oregon 97116

Cover design by Alex Bell

ISBN (pbk) 978-1-945398-09-4
ISBN (epub) 978-1-945398-10-0
ISBN (PDF) 978-1-945398-12-4

Published in the United States of America

Contents

Introduction

Galadriel Chilton

Suddenly he realized what was happening. But by then Harold was over his head in an ocean. He came up thinking fast. And in no time he was climbing aboard a trim little boat. He quickly set sail.

—Crockett Johnson, *Harold and the Purple Crayon*

When I was teaching e-resources management and licensing for the University of Wisconsin, the first required reading was *Harold and the Purple Crayon,* by Crockett Johnson. Harold goes for a moonlit walk and encounters a variety of humorous, and then increasingly frustrating and perilous, situations that he responds to appropriately and quickly with the help of a purple crayon that he uses to draw creative solutions, often with little time to plan. Managing licensed e-resources is similar, and thus requires that one keep a purple crayon and their wits about them.

The goal of this book is to share tips and techniques for managing licensed, commodified e-resources; to help you know what to draw with your purple crayon—to create a connect-the-dots or coloring page of options and resources that you can modify as appropriate to your responsibilities, the resources you manage, and your organization, primarily to make sure that your organization's community can seamlessly access the information it needs. Written by 11 past and present e-resource managers, the text embodies 11 different voices speaking about different parts of managing e-resources; it is meant to be a text that we wish we had had when we suddenly found ourselves in a position of great power requiring a profound amount of responsibility, as described by the American Library Association (2020) in their Library Bill of Rights, first written in 1939: "We significantly influence or control the selection, organization, preservation, and dissemination of information. In a political system grounded in an informed citizenry, we are members of a profession explicitly committed to intellectual freedom and the freedom of access to information."

CITATION

American Library Association. (2020, September 25). Library bill of rights. Retrieved October 18, 2021, from: http://www.ala.org/advocacy/intfreedom/librarybill.

One

What is E-Resource Management in an Academic Library?

Galadriel Chilton

Managing e-resources is the work necessary to ensure that online content—most specifically, the subscriptions and purchases of databases and electronic content (e.g., serials, e-books, etc.) by a library, consortia, or government entity, as well as collected open access content—is acquired, accessible, marketed, evaluated, and renewed or canceled as appropriate to the organization's user community.

This book's issues and frameworks are most applicable to an academic library setting in the United States; however, they may also have some relevance to other library environments. Additionally, given that most e-resources in an academic library are licensed, and that methods for managing paid e-resources are established, this book focuses primarily on commodified e-resources: the online content that academic libraries license and pay to access.

While it's heartening to see the number of open access e-resources grow, along with the methods for enabling open access content, management methods remain varied and transitional. In this book, open access is mentioned throughout (for example, in Chapter 6); however, for more detailed information about managing open access resources, please see *Techniques for Electronic Resource Management: TERMS and the Transition to Open* (Emery, Stone, & McCracken, 2020).

Who does the work of managing e-resources varies at each organization (Macaulay, 2018). Sometimes a single library staff member manages a library's e-resources, while in other situations, an e-resources management team centrally completes the work. At other times or in other organizations, the work is distributed among library staff or even across organizations (e.g., a consortium and a library). Often, the work varies depending on the resource and is a combination of centralized and decentralized tasks.

The day-to-day work of managing e-resources is an unpredictable array of tasks such as troubleshooting sudden or ongoing access issues; working with colleagues to investigate new resources; acquiring content by negotiating licenses, prices, and terms; examining what content should be available and whether it's owned or leased from the content provider; updating access points in a library system to enable users to find and use content (e.g., via a discovery system); collaborating with colleagues on the evaluation and assessment of resources; and liaising with information providers, library colleagues, students, and staff.

However, the care and practice of managing e-resources is paramount to the core of what a library is: a doorway to information to enable a learned society, civil and democratic discourse, and the creation of new knowledge.

With the multitude of e-resources platforms, interfaces, and devices that are now part of the information access equation, it is fundamentally necessary for libraries to provide relevant information to our communities while also ensuring that the users' experience accessing our collections meets or exceeds their expectations. If users cannot easily access what they need, our library collections are irrelevant.

Just as the academy is responsible for supporting freedom of speech and unfettered inquiry, so too are libraries responsible for mitigating the impediments of access so that there is also freedom of access. When libraries purchase content encased in poor interfaces and with impediments to access, it is a form of censorship—a situation that our community is responsible for challenging in the "fulfillment of [our] responsibility to provide information and enlightenment" (American Library Association, 2020).

At most academic institutions, the library typically spends *at least* 75% of their annual collection budget on ongoing subscription content that is nearly all online; thus, staff who manage e-resources have a substantial and significant responsibility (Gremmels, 2013).

E-resource management as a job responsibility or position can be traced back to the 1990s (Duranceau, 2002): No longer were specific, tangible collections bought at a set price, processed, and put on the shelf. Instead, CD-ROMs, and then web-based resources, appeared with recurring fees, terms, and conditions associated with authorized usage, and information providers leased these products rather than sold them to libraries.

As e-resources rapidly became more prevalent, library staff assumed the work of managing them, on the fly, to fulfill a need quickly and with little formal reskilling. Over time, workshops on licensing and conference programs arose to help the library community address key components of the work. Additionally, professional development organizations and library workers began drafting e-resource workflows, lifecycles, and competencies to define the work of e-resources management. Two of the most prominent models are *Core Competencies for E-Resources Librarians*, adopted by NASIG in 2013, and *Techniques for Electronic Resource Management (TERMS)*.

NASIG, which describes itself as "an independent organization working to advance and transform the management of information resources," released its core competencies in 2013. The core competencies provide an excellent overview of the multifaceted work that e-resources management work requires; they serve as a checklist for library administration as competencies that every library should have as an organization via their staff and/or consortia memberships. Additionally, the competencies are a very useful tool for planning and justifying training and staff development that the library as a whole needs in order to appropriately manage e-resource collections.

TERMS 1.0 was developed by and for e-resource managers under the guidance of Jill Emery (Collection Development Librarian, Portland State University) and Graham Stone (Senior Programme Manager for Open Access Monographs, Jisc) in 2008 as "an attempt to create a series of ongoing and continually developing set of management best practices for electronic resource management in libraries" (Emery & Stone, 2013). Working with the e-resources management community, Emery and Stone crowdsourced the development of *TERMS* and worked with Peter McCracken, Electronic Resources Librarian at Cornell University, to develop *TERMS* 2.0 in 2019:

TERMS: Techniques for Electronic Resources Management
http://dx.doi.org/10.5860/ltr.49n2

Techniques for Electronic Resource Management: TERMS and the Transition to Open
https://pdxscholar.library.pdx.edu/ulib_fac/301/

This book was inspired by the *TERMS* 1.0 framework and the need to introduce e-resources management to library staff who are new to this work.

I first realized the importance of this text, when, in fall 2013, my colleague, Chenwei Zhao, and I looked at the course descriptions on websites for ALA-accredited library science programs and reviewed job ads posted on the ALA job list and the ERIL-L and Liblicense-L discussion groups between September and December. For course descriptions, we looked for courses with e-resources management in the title or description, and we looked at collection development course descriptions to see if the description encompassed e-resources, e-journals/packages, e-books, etc. For job ads, it was a small sample and short period of time: 21 ads posted between September and December 2013. This limited sample and time give perspective but review of more ads over a longer period would reveal a clearer, more accurate picture.

Nonetheless, we found that, of the 57 accredited library and information science (LIS) programs, only 19% appeared to have a course that taught the practice and philosophy of managing e-resources, and yet 73% of the job ads posted from September to December 2013 required experience and knowledge of e-resources management. Furthermore, anecdotal reports from colleagues in the field reveal that most see the financial resources spent on e-resources and work to manage these collections continuing to increase while the human resources allocated remain inadequate.

LIS curricula, due to accreditation requirements and review processes, aren't typically able to change as quickly as the e-resources management landscape. The goal of LIS programs is to broadly cover the principles and concepts that librarians can apply to their work in *all* library types and develop their skill set to their evolving work. Additionally, libraries and library organizations should create an appropriately skilled workforce by implementing frameworks and structures for continuity because library staff come from a variety of educational backgrounds and have an array of experiences.

Therefore, it's imperative that academic libraries as organizations develop means to continually build the skills and expertise of their current and new staff to meet the organization's requirements and evolving core competencies. Given the complex nature of the work that is e-resources management, and the large amount of money libraries spend on these needed resources, our hope is that this book will help fill the gaps.

This text provides descriptions, skills, and recommended resources for the following:

- investigating new content for access
- licensing and contracting for e-resource acquisition
- implementing access
- ongoing evaluation and systematic access checks
- annual review

- cancellation and replacement review
- behavioral and communication strategies for e-resources management staff
- trends, challenges, and opportunities in e-resources management
- resources for community and professional development

Throughout this book, as Erika Ripley and Scarlet Galvan note "we have deliberately avoided the use of the word *customer*, favoring *user* instead. *Customer* creates the expectation of a one-off or transactional relationship between the user and library. Libraries provide a suite of services via staff expertise for an active, participatory user community. By contrast, as consumers of resources, *customers* are not active participants in the systems a library maintains. We have also favored *library staff* over *librarian* because many individuals conduct the functional work of the library regardless of credentials or title."

Each chapter is written by a past or present manager of e-resources and/or an e-resource licensing expert, and each chapter's author brings their own voice to their practice of this important work.

CITATIONS

American Library Association. (2020, September 25). Library bill of rights. Retrieved October 18, 2021, from: http://www.ala.org/advocacy/intfreedom/librarybill.

Daniel, K., Esposito, J. J., & Schonfeld, R. C. (2019). *Library acquisition patterns.* https://doi.org/10.18665/sr.310937

Duranceau, E. F. (2002). Staffing for electronic resource management: The results of a survey. *Serials Review, 28*(4), 316–320. https://doi.org/0.1016/S0098-7913(02)00224-1

Emery, J., & Stone, G. (2013). *Techniques for electronic resource management.* Chicago: ALA TechSource. https://doi.org/10.5860/ltr.49n2

Emery, J., Stone, G., & McCracken, P. (2020). *Techniques for electronic resource management: TERMS and the transition to open.* Chicago: American Library Association. https://pdxscholar.library.pdx.edu/ulib_fac/301/

Gremmels, G. S. (2013). Staffing trends in college and university libraries. *Reference Services Review, 41*(2), 233–252. https://doi.org/10.1108/00907321311326165

Macaulay, D. (2018). Sharing the load: Distribution of electronic resources management responsibilities among U.S. academic librarians, *Serials Review, 44*(4), 259–274, https://doi.org/10.1080/00987913.2018.1553089

NASIG. (2013). *NASIG core competencies for electronic resources librarians.* https://www.nasig.org/Competencies-Eresources

Two

Glossary of Terms

Galadriel Chilton

Note: This glossary builds on collaborative work by Chenwei Zhao and Galadriel Chilton.

As with all professions, libraries are full of terms, acronyms, and jargon used among staff as a means of communicating concepts. E-resource management, as a specific area of library work, has its own rich vocabulary of terms that e-resources staff use amongst themselves, to communicate with vendors and publishers, to communicate with staff, and for record-keeping.

Some of the terms below are format agnostic, used across library departments (e.g., acquisitions, cataloging, etc.), and some are unique to e-resources. Additionally, though this book focuses on commodified e-resources, open access terms are included for general reference.

Access Title

A journal title that is accessible with paid fees, but for which access ends once the library ceases payment. See also *Cross Access.*

All or Nothing

A package comprised of publisher-selected titles and that includes all the publisher-selected titles only.

Annual Access Fee

A fee paid to continue access to a *One-Time Purchase* on the vendor/ publisher's platform. Typically, the annual access fees are lower than the initial purchase price. Also known as a *Hosting Fee* or *Continuing Service Fee.*

Approval Plan

Like a *standing order,* a method of acquiring content whereby the vendor automatically sends materials (typically single-title/single-volume materials or book series' such as print or e-books) to the library based on predetermined criteria like subject, publisher, and so on. Libraries pay only for titles that they accept and add to their collection. They return titles that they don't keep.

Authentication

Verification of identity or verification that a user is who they claim to be. Example authentication methods include Athens, IP Address, EZProxy, and Shibboleth.

Authorization

Rules that determine who is allowed to access what. For paid e-resources, authorized users are typically the academic institution's students, faculty, staff, and walk-in users, with select authorization granted to visiting scholars, alumni, and so on.

Available Titles

All of a publisher's available titles, including those to which a library subscribes, and to which *Authorized Users* have access, <u>*as well as*</u> a publisher's titles that a library neither subscribes nor has access to.

Backfile

Older volumes and issues of a journal that a library may or may not have access to as part of its subscription. Backfiles may only be available via a purchase separate from the subscription fees to the *Frontfile* or current content. See also *Frontfile.*

Big Deal

When print journals became available online, larger publishers began offering journal packages that included electronic access to a large portion of the publisher's *Available Titles.* The pricing for these bundles was based on a library's past spend on print subscriptions from that publisher. "'The Big Deal' usually allows the library to cancel paper subscriptions at some savings or purchase additional paper copies at discounted prices. But the content is, henceforth, 'bundled' so that individual journal subscriptions can no longer be canceled in their electronic format" (Frazier, 2001).

Bridge Agreement

A limited-term amendment to an executed, but expired, license; enacted to afford more negotiation time for a new license.

Cancellation Allowance

For journal packages, how many titles or how much of the total spend a library can cancel. Typically, the cancellation allowance for publisher packages—if available—is noted in the license agreement. Most often, cancellation allowances are a percentage of the total subscription fee (e.g., 2% of the total package fees).

CLOCKSS

A dark archive of scholarly content (https://www.clockss.org/clockss /Home). Content no longer available from any publisher is freely available. See also *LOCKSS* and *Portico.*

Continuing Service Fee

See *Annual Access Fee.*

Core Titles

See *Subscribed Titles.*

COUNTER

Counting Online Usage of Networked Electronic Resources is a Code of Practice for recording and reporting usage statistics for e-resources: (http://www.projectcounter.org/about.html).

CORAL

A freely available, open-source *Electronic Resource Management System* (http://coral-erm.org/).

Cross Access Fee

A fee paid to access content for a specific *License Term*; there is no perpetual access to journals available via cross access. Access fees are typically for a package of titles and less than they would be for a subscription; they are analogous to fees a library paid for access to an aggregate database. *Example:* Elsevier's Freedom Collection.

Cross Access Titles

Titles accessible because institutions pay a cross access fee and/or because a library is part of a consortial deal, and part of the deal includes cross access to titles subscribed to by all other libraries in the deal.

Database Model

Like a *Package Deal*, a set subscription fee the library pays for a predetermined package of journals. Usually, no swapping of titles or cancellations of single journals is permitted. See also *Lump Sum* and *Big Deal.*

DOI

A **D**igital **O**bject **I**dentifier is an International Organization for Standardization standard for a unique and persistent handle to identify objects.

Embargo

A period in which content (e.g., a journal article) is not available for access via a library's subscription and/or on a platform. Typically, an embargo impacts the most recently published content. Embargo periods can be in months (e.g., three, six, or 12 months) or years (e.g., one year, three years).

Entitlement List

A publisher-generated list of journal titles to which a library has access. This list often includes *Subscribed Titles* and *Cross Access Titles.*

Electronic Resource Management System (ERMS)

An app—freestanding or part of the ILS—specifically for managing e-resources.

Firm Order

The order and acquisition of a single item by title, typically a book, e-book, video or audio stream.

Frontfile

Current volumes and issues of a journal that a library can or does subscribe to. Frontfiles are typically a separate subscription from access to unsubscribed backfiles. See also *Backfile.*

FTE

Full-time equivalent. Frequently, FTE is a component to determine a library's price for a given e-resource. Examples include using FTE as a multiplier, e.g. $1 per FTE, or basing price on a sized-based tier (e.g. Carnegie Size & Setting Classification, https://carnegieclassifications.iu.edu/classi-fication_descriptions/size_setting.php).

Holdings

The *Subscribed Titles* and *Access Titles* available to a specific library, with details about the range of volumes and dates that the library can access.

Hosting Fee

See *Annual Access Fee.*

Integrated Library System (ILS)

Also known as a *Library Management System,* an ILS is the industry-spe-cific enterprise system that libraries use to manage their operations. An ILS has a backend interface for staff as well as a user interface for library users.

IP Address

An **I**nternet **P**rotocol address is the sequence of numbers assigned to each device (e.g., computer, tablet, cell phone) that connects to the internet or to a computer network that uses the Internet Protocol.

ISSN

An **I**nternational **S**tandard **S**erial **N**umber is an internationally agreed-upon standard number that uniquely identifies a serial publication. In the U.S., ISSNs are assigned by the Library of Congress, and a pub-lication can have different ISSNs based on format (e.g., print journal, electronic journal).

Jumper

A journal that jumps from one publisher to another. See also *Transfer Title.*

Library Management System

See *Integrated Library System (ILS)*.

License

The legal agreement between the publisher and the library and/or the consortia governing the term, fees, use, access, etc. of e-resources. See Chapter 4: Acquiring New Content: The Joy of Licensing and Contracting for E-Resource Acquisition.

License Term

The length of time that a license covers (e.g., one year, five years, perpetual).

LOCKSS

Lots of Copies Keep Stuff Safe is a collaborative digital preservation initiative (http://www.lockss.org/). See also *Portico and CLOCKSS*.

Lump Sum

Like a *Package Deal* or *Database Model* in which a library purchases a package of journals for one fee; title-specific prices aren't included on the journal title list. However, swaps may be allowed. See also *Big Deal*.

MARC

Machine-readable cataloging. Library staff use MARC standards—a set of digital formats—to create descriptive catalog records for library materials.

Moving vs. Fixed Wall Access

A moving wall rolls forward in time, always preventing the most recent years from showing. A fixed wall stops materials at a particular date, usually because the publisher has their own materials available from that moment in time. Some publishers don't make recent content available due to concern that making such content available would hurt print publication sales or because electronic access is exclusively available via another provider. JSTOR is one example of a product with fixed and moving walls, as is ProQuest's Historical New York Times. See also *Embargo.*

One-Time Purchase
An e-resource that institutions pay for with one fee for perpetual access. To maintain access via the vendor or publisher's interface, an *Annual Access Fee* is typically required.

Open Access (OA)
Content which is available for free to access and access does not require affiliation with a library or any other means of authentication or authorization. Open Access content typically includes additional rights, such as permitting redistribution, reproduction, and modification.

Open Educational Resources (OER)
Open-access, freely available, and accessible text, media, and other content (usually digital) for teaching, learning, and research purposes.

Open Movement
In libraries, the "Open Movement" typically refers to promoting *Open Access* and *Open Educational Resources.*

Order Type
The type of e-journal subscription acquired: *Package Deal, Title-by-Title, Subscribed Titles* only, or *Subscribed Titles + Cross Access Titles.* See also *Pricing Model.*

Package Deal
A package of journals that includes only a predetermined list of journals for a set subscription fee. The swapping of titles or the cancellation of a

single journal is usually permitted. See also *Big Deal, Database Model* and *Lump Sum.*

Permalink

A URL that is intended to remain static and unchanged. Platforms often have a tool to get permalinks for articles, chapters, and other content.

Perpetual Access

The continued access to subscribed content even when a subscription to current content ceases. Also known as Perpetual Rights. See also *Post-Cancellation Access.*

Perpetual License

The continuing right to access *Subscribed Titles* after the termination of a subscription to current content. Also, a license with no termination or end date.

Perpetual Rights

See *Perpetual Access.*

PORTICO

A membership-supported digital archive that preserves access to e-journals, e-books, and other scholarly electronic content (http://www.portico.org/digital-preservation/).

Post-Cancellation Access

Access to *Subscribed Titles* after subscription cancellation. Post-cancellation access can include online access via the vendor or publisher's platform or via storage media (e.g., DVD, external hard drive, etc.) that the vendor or publisher provides to the library upon cancellation. See also *Perpetual Access.*

Pricing Model

How the pricing is determined for the package, such as *Title-by-Title* or *Lump Sum.*

Proxy Server

A server application that is an intermediary for requests from users seeking to access content from content's server. For example, a user seeking access to a library e-resource from off campus will be using a computer without a campus IP address and thus is not an authorized user of the library's e-resources until the user authenticates through a proxy server so that it appears to the content's server that the user is accessing the e-resource with an institutional IP address. EZProxy, owned by OCLC, is an example of a web proxy server that authenticates users' access to a library's e-resources by IP address.

PURL

Persistent **URL** and a kind of *Permalink.*

Read and Publish

A kind of *Transformative Agreement.*

Renewal Frequency

How often subscriptions are reviewed and renewed. For most journal subscriptions, renewals occur every 12 months, and the *Subscription Period* is from January to December.

Serial

A publication in any format, released in continuing installments or successive parts and including numeric or chronological designations, and intended to be continued indefinitely. Serials include periodicals; newspapers; annuals (reports, yearbooks, etc.); the journals, memoirs, proceedings, transactions, and so on of societies; and numbered monographic series.

SERU

Shared **E-R**esource **U**nderstanding is a National Information Standards Organization (NISO) best practice that, when implemented by a library and vendor, sets standard business practices for e-resource use and access (https://www.niso.org/standards-committees/seru). Because copyright law governs use, no license is required.

Signature Authority

A person in a position with signature authority is one who can sign legal documents on behalf of an institution or organization. In libraries, signature authority to sign license agreements is usually limited to library directors or deans, and the value of the license may dictate who has signature authority. *Do not sign a license agreement or any other legal document unless you have written documentation outlining your authority to do so.*

Simultaneous Users (SU)

The number of users who can use an e-resource at one time. Some e-resources, especially e-books, limit simultaneous users to one, three, five, etc., user(s) at a time. An e-resource with unlimited simultaneous users has no limits on how many users can access the content at one time.

Spend

The minimum amount that must be paid, either annually or for *License Term.*

Standing Order

An order placed by a library with a publisher, jobber, or dealer to supply each volume or part of a specific title or type of publication as it is published, until further notice. Unlike subscriptions, which must be paid in advance, standing orders are billed as each volume is shipped. Sometimes used synonymously with continuation order.

Subscribed Titles

Titles for which a library pays a subscription fee and, as a result, has access. Under some licenses, Subscribed Titles provide *Perpetual Access* for the volumes and issues for which subscription fees were paid.

Subscription Agent

A firm or organization that arranges, at the order of an individual or library, for the regular delivery of serials as they are published and handles the financial records. For example, EBSCO, Harrassowitz, WT Cox, etc.

Subscription Period

The subscription term. Typically 12 months on the calendar year (January through December).

Swap

Prior to the annual renewal of a journal package, the taking out of one journal title and replacing it with another journal title available from the same publisher. In order for the swap to occur, the subscription cost for the title(s) added must be same or greater than the subscription fee for the title(s) removed.

Swap Allowance

The clause of a journal package license that describes the terms, conditions, and limits of swapping titles in and out of the package upon annual renewal.

Title-by-Title

A package in which a library pays subscription fees on a title-by-title basis.

Typically, journal titles can be *Swapped*, provided that the total subscription fees or *Spend* remains the same or higher.

Transfer Title
A title that moves from one publisher to another. See also *Jumper.*

Transfer Code of Practice
A NISO standard that provides guidelines for transferring and receiving publishers of *Transfer Titles* to help library staff manage access to journal content (https://www.niso.org/standards-committees/transfer).

Transformative Agreement
A license agreement for content (typically journals) that aims to shift a library's payment away from subscription access for *Authorized Users* only to *Open Access* (Hinchliffe, 2019).

Unsubscribed Titles
Titles to which a library does not subscribe but to which it may have access as part of a negotiated deal, particularly a consortium deal. See also *Cross Access Titles.*

Voluntary Product Accessibility Template (VPAT)
A VPAT "is a document that explains how information and communication technology (ICT) products such as software, hardware, electronic content, and support documentation meet (conform to) the Revised 508 Standards for IT accessibility" (U.S. General Services Administration, 2018).

CITATIONS

Frazier, K. (2001). The librarians' dilemma: Contemplating the costs of the "Big Deal." *D-Lib Magazine, 7*(3). http://www.dlib.org/dlib/march01/frazier/03frazier.html

Hinchliffe, L. J. (2019, April 23). Transformative agreements: A primer. *The Scholarly*

Kitchen. https://scholarlykitchen.sspnet.org/2019/04/23/transformative
-agreements/

U.S. General Services Administration. (2018, April). Voluntary product accessibility template (VPAT). *Section508.gov.* https://www.section508.gov/sell/vpat/

Three

Investigating New Content for Access

Galadriel Chilton

A basic framework should be considered with every new purchase or addition to content that is selected for inclusion into the 21st-century library.

—TERMS

In the *TERMS* section entitled "Investigation of New Content," the authors detail six foundational steps for investigating new content:

1. Know what you want to achieve
2. Write your specification document
3. Get the right team
4. Do a desktop review of market and literature and then a trial setup
5. Talk to suppliers or vendors
6. Make your choice
   (Emery & Stone, 2013)

Building on *TERMS*, this chapter focuses on e-resources for which a library pays for access, either as a perpetual access purchase or a subscription. Additionally, see Appendix A at the end of this chapter for a checklist to modify as appropriate for your institution and your library's workflows.

ACQUIRING E-RESOURCES: QUESTIONS TO CONSIDER

A library's acquisition of e-resources encompasses many variables, due to different pricing sources, formats (e.g., database, e-journal, e-book, dataset, streaming media, etc.), licenses, payees, interfaces, and access options. Investigating e-resources for acquisition means that it's necessary to evaluate the content and interface as well as the technological and legal concerns.

Content is incredibly important and usually the primary driver in exploring acquisition of new content; however, it isn't the only deciding factor, because the content has no value if those seeking it cannot use it, or if users choose not to use it because of a difficult, inaccessible interface—just as the most amazing destination is lost without a clear means of arrival. In some cases, content in a subscription database may be freely available, but the free user interface significantly impedes access, and/or the subscription interface introduces new desirable ways to access, use, and interact with the content.

To aid with evaluating the content and user interface of an e-resource, most vendors offer trials, allowing library staff and the potential primary users of the resource to freely evaluate its content and usability for a specific period. Trials can be invaluable for assessing a potential e-resource; however, because managing trials also requires staff time, it's worth developing a trial policy, as part of or adjacent to the library's collection development policy, that incorporates factors such as:

- criteria for who may request a trial and when
- when trials are run (at what time of year are the potential users most likely to provide feedback?)
- who will craft and who will distribute messaging to the users about the trial
- what kind of mechanism is in place to gather and consider user feedback

In their presentation at the 2012 Electronic Resources & Libraries conference entitled *Trials by Juries: Suggested Practices for Database Trials,* Adams et al. discuss good basic questions and criteria about starting trial access for e-resources, including curricular relevance of the resource, trial access methods, marketing and communication, trial evaluation, decision-making, and record keeping (Adams et al., 2012).

An additional recommendation for trials is that communication to users include a brief note explaining that all e-resource acquisitions must be in accordance with the library's principles and values, including licenses and terms of use. Proactively communicating licensing values to users helps them understand the complicated e-resource landscape that libraries navigate for access.

Beyond the content and user interface evaluations via literature reviews, trials, and staff review, library staff should also evaluate and consider aspects of managing the e-resource within the context of their country's laws, as well as institutional and library policies (e.g., collection development policies) and values such as but not limited to:

- access and authentication
- accessibility for those with disabilities
- authorized use and academic freedom
- user privacy
- licensing terms (see more in the next chapter)
- administrative interface
- technical support

Furthermore, important questions to consider include but are not limited to:

- What does it look like when you apply your library's collection development or management policies and values to e-resource acquisitions?
  - For example: Is access to content imperative and does it override

    user privacy, or is a vendor's collection of user information or lack of a secure connection to the e-resource a deal breaker?

- What is the context driving the acquisition?
  - For example: Does the e-resource support a new curriculum or accreditation?

Given that all libraries have limited resources—both funding to pay for and human resources to manage an e-resource collection—answering the above questions and others specific to your library will help you prioritize which e-resource acquisitions to pursue.

    Beyond your institution's local policies, are there frameworks that are appropriate to apply to investigating and evaluating resources? Two examples include:

- MIT's *Framework for Publisher Contracts* (2020)
- NERL's *Preferred Deal Elements for License Negotiations* (2021)

ACCESS AND AUTHENTICATION

At this time, at the end of 2021, most e-resources are accessible on and off campus by authenticated users via the authentication method implemented by the library and/or parent institution (e.g., VPN or proxy server). However, some specialized e-resources are accessible only on campus and authenticated only through a specific username and password, or require a user to create an account with their institutional email address.

    Such specialized access and authentication typically mean that it will take more library staff time to manage and make the e-resource accessible. This extra time is worth noting and may be a valid negotiation point. For example, because subscribing to the resource requires more of the subscribing institution's time compared to similar e-resource subscriptions, what is the best price the vendor can offer?

ACCESSIBILITY FOR THOSE WITH DISABILITIES

Even though e-resources are hosted on platforms and servers outside of the library, libraries are still legally responsible for ensuring that e-resources provided through the library are accessible to users with disabilities. Therefore, understanding the e-resource's accessibility is a key part of investigating an e-resource for acquisition.

The Big Ten Academic Alliance (BTAA) formed a Library E-Resource Accessibility Group in 2015 to investigate, and investigate concerns about, e-resource accessibility, such as VPAT availability and compliance. BTAA created a Library Accessibility Toolkit (https://www.btaa.org/library/reports/library-e-resource-accessibility--testing) and drafted and adopted model accessibility language for e-resource licenses. The toolkit includes already-created tools and resources as well as an open invitation for further contributions.

AUTHORIZED USE, ACADEMIC FREEDOM, AND USER PRIVACY

While evaluating the content and interface of an e-resource, it's also important to evaluate the terms of use and the license terms, if the resource would be acquired from a new vendor or under a different license and terms than other e-resources acquired by the same vendor. Chapter 4 explores licenses in greater detail, and during the evaluation process, it's important to understand whether the license will meet your library's and institution's criteria. Waiting until after an initial evaluation and successful trial to review the license, only to find egregious deal breakers, could lead to disappointed users.

It is imperative to understand both your library's and institution's policies and procedures about authorized use, academic freedom, and user privacy—some of which may be in place due to state or federal laws (e.g., in the United States, the Family Educational Rights and Privacy Act, or FERPA). Some institutions may have state-specific or locally created appendices or riders that vendors must agree to and append to every e-resource license agreement. If such policies aren't readily available, working with library colleagues to establish them is highly recommended for consistent and efficient negotiation with vendors on these issues.

Article VII of the Library Bill of Rights states, "All people, regardless of origin, age, background, or views, possess a right to privacy and confidentiality in their library use. Libraries should advocate for, educate about, and protect people's privacy, safeguarding all library use data, including personally identifiable information" (American Library Association, 2019), but the internet and e-resources designed and hosted by entities outside the library complicate matters significantly.

In her blog post titled "Libraries no longer guard patron privacy," Dorothea Salo notes that "neither public nor academic libraries make much, if any, effort to prevent third-party tracking of internet use from library computers, never mind library-provided Wi-Fi" and also notes that "e-resource vendors from whom libraries purchase access also routinely track patron information use and are trying to do so more commonly and more identifiably" (Salo, 2019).

In his presentation at the 2019 Center for Networked Information (CNI) membership meeting, Cody Hanson noted, "I do not believe it is possible for use of licensed resources to be private," after sharing his findings that "on average, each publisher site had 18 third-party assets being loaded on their article pages" (Hanson, 2018).

Given Salo's and Hanson's findings, understanding your institution's practices and policies, as well as your library's values, and then working with library and institution colleagues (e.g., IT, general counsel) is important practice that should be part of the evaluation of, and negotiation for, e-resources with regard to your users' privacy.

ADMINISTRATIVE INTERFACE AND LIBRARY BRANDING

Alongside their evaluation of an e-resource's content, user interface, and license, library staff must also investigate whether they will have access to an administrative interface for managing the e-resource. Common functionality in an admin interface includes the ability to set user interface display options, such as basic/advanced search, brief/detailed results views, etc., as well as the ability to brand the e-resource as being provided by the library.

As the Columbia University Libraries note, "library branding is more important than the vendor's or publisher's corporate brands" (Columbia University Libraries, n.d.a). In the Libraries' collection development policies and strategies, the section titled *The libraries' expectations of collections vendors* includes:

- the Libraries expects the option to place prominent branding (preferably a Columbia University Libraries banner) on vendor and publisher pages and services, per the options and requirements outlined by the Libraries;
- advertising should not be placed on pages or services associated with library resources. For the avoidance of doubt, this does not include advertising that is part of the content itself, such as ads found within journals, magazines, archival or primary source material, etc.
- the Libraries' banner should be the main and largest branding/logo on the page;
- the Libraries' banner should have top left presence, above any vendor, publisher, or product logos or branding;
- the Libraries' banner should be accessible across all pages of the e-resource(s);
- the Libraries' banner should be clickable back to Libraries' home page, http://library.columbia.edu/.
- a link to "Ask a Columbia Librarian" should be on the site, http://

www.columbia.edu/cgi-bin/cul/resolve?lweb0031.
(Columbia University Libraries, n.d.b)

If your library does not yet have expectations in place for collections vendors and publishers, developing them will help with efficient and consistent negotiations.

ACQUISITION: FOUR DETERMINATIONS

There are four factors of the acquisition to consider, both as part of the decision-making process and after your library decides to acquire an e-resource:

- price
- license
- payee
- access

Each e-resource may have one option for each factor, or a different option for each. Let's investigate each factor in more detail:

Price

Your library's price for an e-resource could vary depending on who is issuing the offer. For example, the price could come directly from the vendor who created the e-resource, but it also might come from the vendor's billing agent or a subscription agent working on behalf of the vendor or content creator, or it could be a price offered by a library consortium.

License

Just like price, the license agreement can come from multiple parties. It could be that a library consortium has already negotiated a license with the vendor on behalf of its membership, or the license could be what a vendor or the vendor's agent offers, or you could work at a library that has a master license agreement.

Payee

After completing license and price negotiation, an invoice is issued; however, it may or may not be issued by the vendor. Your library's invoice may come from a consortium, a subscription agent, the vendor, a billing agent working on behalf of the vendor, a third-party host, or from another organization with whom your library shares the cost of the e-resource.

Access Options

Access information and the e-resource platform may be from the vendor or from a third party.

Examples

So, what does it look like to have different factors for different e-resources? Let's walk through a couple of examples. First, here are the options for each of the factors:

A. Determine Price	B. Determine License	C. Determine Payee	D. Access Options
1. Consortium 2. Subscription agent 3. Vendor direct 4. Vendor's billing agent	1. Consortium 2. Vendor direct 3. Vendor's agent 4. Library master license	1. Consortium 2. Vendor direct 3. Subscription agent 4. Vendor's billing Agent 5. Third-party host 6. Cost-share with other entity	1. Vendor direct 2. Third-party platform

Let's consider your library's purchase of the fictitious **Sapphire Journal Package**. The price is determined by a consortium negotiation, the license is negotiated between the library and vendor (Sapphire), the invoice and payee are the vendor, and access is directly through the vendor's platform. So you have:

Sapphire Journal Package: A1, B2, C2, D1:

A. Determine Price	B. Determine License	C. Determine Payee	D. Access Options
1. **Consortium** 2. Subscription agent 3. Vendor direct 4. Vendor's billing agent	1. Consortium 2. **Vendor direct** 3. Vendor's agent 4. Library master license	1. Consortium 2. **Vendor direct** 3. Subscription agent 4. Vendor's billing agent 5. Third-party host 6. Cost-share with other entity	1. **Vendor direct** 2. Third-party platform

Here's another example, for a subscription to the make-believe **Ultra Premier Academic Database**, where the price and license terms are determined by your library's direct negotiation with the vendor, as are the payee and access options:

The **Ultra Premier Academic Database**: A3, B2, C2, D1

A. Determine Price	B. Determine License	C. Determine Payee	D. Access Options
1. Consortium 2. Subscription agent 3. **Vendor**	1. Consortium 2. **Vendor direct** 3. Vendor's	1. Consortium 2. **Vendor direct** 3. Subscription agent	1. **Vendor direct** 2. Third-party platform

direct 4. Vendor's billing agent	agent 4. Library master license	4. Vendor's billing agent 5. Third-party host 6. Cost-share with other entity	

One more example is the **Ruby Journals Package**, where the price is negotiated by a consortium on behalf of the library, but the parties to the license are the library and the vendor, and the payee is a subscription agent. Additionally, the subscription cost is shared (e.g., the university's health sciences library sends funds to the mail library to help pay for the subscription).

Ruby Journals Package: A1, B2, C3+C6, D1

A. Determine Price	B. Determine License	C. Determine Payee	D. Access Options
1. **Consortium** 2. Subscription agent 3. Vendor direct 4. Vendor's billing agent	1. Consortium 2. **Vendor direct** 3. Vendor's agent 4. Library master license	1. Consortium 2. Vendor direct 3. **Subscription agent** 4. Vendor's billing agent 5. Third-party host 6. **Cost-share with other entity**	1. **Vendor direct** 2. Third-party platform

CONCLUSION

The questions to ask and criteria to consider before acquiring an e-resource are numerous and complicated—many of the questions might have "yes and no" answers or be inconclusive. All of this may seem like a lot and be overwhelming, and it's a significant amount of important work. However, taking time to develop frameworks and practices for consistency and efficiency will help save time in the long run, and, most importantly, help ensure that your library's e-resource collection is well-developed and supports your users.

CITATIONS AND FURTHER READING

Branding of E-Resources

Columbia University Libraries. (n.d.a). E-resource branding. Behind the Scenes: Collection Development & Electronic Resources Management. https://library.columbia.edu/bts/cerm/e-resource-branding.html

Columbia University Libraries. (n.d.b). *The libraries' expectations of collections vendors.* Collection Development Policies & Strategies. https://library.columbia.edu/about/policies/collection-development-policies-strategies.html

Evaluating E-Resources for Potential Acquisition

Adams A. L., Ritterbush, J., & Ryan, C. E. (2012, April 3). *Trials by juries: Suggested practices for database trials.* Electronic Resources & Libraries, Austin, TX. https://www.slideshare.net/LibrariLee/trials-by-juries-lee-ritterbushryan

Johnson, S., Evensen, O. G., Gelfand, J., Lammers, G., Sipe, L., & Zilper, N. (2012, August). *Key issues for e-resource collection development: A guide for libraries.* IFLA Acquisition and Development Section. https://www.ifla.org/files/assets/acquisition-collection-development/publications/electronic-resource-guide-en.pdf

Yue, P. W. (2016). Using technology to facilitate pre-acquisition workflows for electronic resources. *Proceedings of the Charleston Library Conference.* http://dx.doi.org/10.5703/1288284316555

Frameworks for E-Resource Acquisitions

Emery, J. & Stone, G. (2013). Investigating new content for addition/purchase. *TERMS: Techniques for Electronic Resource Management.* Chicago: ALA TechSource. https://doi.org/10.5860/ltr.49n2

MIT Ad Hoc Task Force on Open Access to MIT's Research, MIT Faculty Committee on the Library System, & MIT Libraries. (2020, May 19). *MIT framework for publisher contracts.* Scholarly Publishing—MIT Libraries. https://libraries.mit.edu/scholarly/publishing/framework/

Stamison, C. (2021, May 26). *NERL develops preferred deal elements for license negotiations.* NERL. http://nerl.org/2021/05/26/nerl-develops-preferred-deal-elements/

E-Resource Accessibility

Big Ten Academic Alliance. (n.d.). Testing. *Library E-Resource Accessibility.* https://www.btaa.org/library/reports/library-e-resource-accessibility--testing

Fernandez, M. (2018). How accessible is our collection? Performing an e-resources accessibility review. *The Serials Librarian, 74*(1-4), 81–86. https://doi.org/10.1080/036152 6X.2018.1430424

Privacy

American Library Association. (2019, January 29). *Library bill of rights.* https://www.ala .org/advocacy/intfreedom/librarybill

Hanson, C. (2018, April 8–9). *User tracking on publisher platforms.* Coalition for Networked Information Spring 2019 Member Meeting, St. Louis, Missouri. https://www.codyh .com/writing/tracking.html

Salo, D. (2019, April 11). Libraries no longer guard patron privacy. *Dorothea Salo.* https:// dsalo.info/libraries-no-longer-guard-patron-privacy/

APPENDIX A: CHECKLIST FOR INVESTIGATING NEW CONTENT

Notes:

1. The following checklist is based on the TERMS Checklist for Investigating New Content for Purchase/Addition and is used here in accordance with its Creative Commons license.

2. This is a very general list and is intended to be a starting point. Applying this checklist to your organization's process for investigating a potential e-resource acquisition requires a collaborative effort and expertise from across the library staff.

CONTENT

Task / Question	Who will complete this task/ answer this question?
• Does the resource's content align with the library's collection development policy?	
• Does the resource's content align with diversity, equity, and inclusion in collections?	
• Who is the intended audience?	

Is there a potential bias based on:	
◦ undergraduate or postgraduate bias?	
◦ geographic location (e.g., northern hemisphere, southern hemisphere)?	
◦ gender, race, etc.?	
• Is the resource required for accreditation?	
• What do authoritative reviews note about the resource?	
If the resource has duplicate coverage of an existing resource or freely available content:	
◦ What are the results of the overlap analysis?	
◦ How does the user interface compare in terms of ease of access?	
◦ Are there justifiable reasons to acquire despite results of overlap analysis?	
• Does the resource include cover-to-cover full text (e.g., all articles, advertisements, commentary, letters to the editor, etc.) or is it selective? If selective, will the selective content meet user need?	
• What is the ratio of current content to ceased or halted coverage?	
• What publishers are covered? Are they varied and diverse in terms of content, publication place, etc.?	

COST

Task / Question	Who will complete this task/ answer this question?
• What are the initial setup/one-time costs?	
• What are the setup time estimates?	
• What are the ongoing costs and maintenance requirements?	
• Are price increases limited to a certain percent each year?	
• Is this a one-year or multiyear contract?	
• Are discounts available?	
• Is the cost over time sustainable given budget trends?)	
• Are there extra costs or discounts for multiple locations?	

INTERFACE

Task / Question	Who will complete this task/ answer this question?
• If the content is available from more than one vendor or via more than one interface, which interface is preferred by users and most accessible to those with disabilities?	
• Is the interface intuitive for the primary users?	
Does the resource work well...	

◦ with multiple browsers (i.e., Brave, Firefox, Chrome, Microsoft Edge, Safari)?	
◦ on mobile devices?	
• Does the resource have text-to-speech capability, closed captioning, and other tools for accessibility?	
• What are the resource's unique features?	

ACCESS & LICENSE

Task / Question	Who will complete this task/ answer this question?
• Is access restricted to a certain number of concurrent users, or is access unlimited?	
• Is access restricted by location (e.g., on campus only)?	
• Is the resource indexed in a discovery service such as Primo, WorldShare, etc.?	
• Does the resource work with EZproxy, etc., for authenticating users?	
• Does the resource meet our license requirements for authorization, authentication, and access? (see Chapter 4)	
• What are the vendor's policies around tracking and collecting user data? Do these policies and practices violate our library's	

and/or institution's policies?	

ADMINISTRATION

Task / Question	Who will complete this task/ answer this question?

• Are e-resource usage statistics available?
   ◦ What is the process for getting the statistics?
   ◦ Are usage statistics COUNTER compliant?	

• Is there a library administration portal?	
• Is training provided for library staff or students? ◦ Is there a cost? (If so, consider negotiating training into the license as part of the subscription fee at no extra charge.)	

SPECIAL CONSIDERATIONS FOR E-BOOKS

Task / Question	Who will complete this task/ answer this question?
• MARC records? Note: It's worth asking for a sample set of MARC records for review by cataloging and metadata staff to evaluate for quality and e-book discovery.	
• Access after cancellation	
• Process for deleting/weeding	

SPECIAL CONSIDERATIONS FOR E-JOURNALS

Task / Question	Who will complete this task/ answer this question?
• Access after cancellation (e.g., Portico)	

Four

The Joy of Licensing and Contracting for E-Resource Acquisition

Joan M. Emmet

If someone asks you to purchase or subscribe to e-resources for your organization, then you may need to review and sign the license agreement for those e-resources. Typically, the information provider or publisher offers you an agreement rather than using your own license or a model agreement (more on model agreements later). In fact, you may simply sign it, not thinking twice that the document is negotiable for better terms and reduced liability or risk.

We have all encountered shrink-wrap or click-through agreements in our personal lives that require us to accept the terms or else we cannot use the product. Rarely do most of us read the terms of those apparently binding agreements. With license agreements, it is well worth your time, as the license reviewer, to read the entire document or documents and understand the laws governing such agreements. Doing so gives the best chance to avoid liability for your organization and permits the broadest and most beneficial use terms for your users. We'll start this chapter with some definitions, a review of the law, and an analysis to identify potential red-flag sections, and we'll apply this awareness to modify sections and language of actual agreements. Then we'll cover license construction, negotiation, and other alternatives. The chapter closes with two appendixes of materials to include in a reviewer's toolkit for easy reference:

- checklists identifying language to scrutinize

- useful sample language to copy and paste into existing agreements

DEFINING THE LICENSE

License and Copyright

The document you receive will usually comprise pages of text that are packed full of confusing words we know as "legalese." You may want to postpone reading or decide to just sign because you don't really know what this language means or the consequences it may engender. Below, we will take apart some confusing aspects of the document to help you understand which elements need the closest attention.

License

What is a license? Simply put, the license is what permits you and your organization the right to use the content in certain ways that might otherwise violate someone's copyright interest. It means that the licensor (the entity leasing the content to your organization) may grant the licensee (your organization) and the licensee's users certain permissions for uses that only the copyright owner holds. We associate these rights with various types of use, such as copying, distributing, making new works based on the original (derivatives), performing, or displaying (Copyright Act of 1976, 2021). In a nutshell, that is what the license is all about. The document you receive may permit or prohibit some of these uses. The licensee and its users must simply abide by the terms of use outlined in the agreement.

But wait, there's more. Almost always included in the document are contractual obligations above and beyond the granting of use rights. These obligations apply to both parties and may even try to loop in third parties (the authorized users or platform/content providers) who aren't even party to the agreement! While typically, your organization is referred to as the "licensee" and the vendor is the "licensor" in these agreements, other terms might be used instead, such as "subscriber," "buyer," or "purchaser," or the exact name of your entity, and "provider" or "seller," or even simply the name of the licensing entity. Whatever the terms, it all amounts to the same thing and should be made consistent throughout an agreement.

Following the Law: Copyright

We need to inspect each part of the agreement, so let us begin with the portion that is governed both by copyright law and contract law. First, let's review some elements of copyright. Title 17 of the U.S. Code, Section 101 *et seq.* codifies copyright law and provides users of others' copyrighted works certain rights because of Congress's interpretation of the Constitution. U.S. copyright law began in the Constitution, which granted Congress the power "to promote the progress of science and useful arts, by securing for **limited times** to authors and inventors the exclusive right to their respective writings and discoveries" (U.S. Const. art. I, § 8). In fact, today's copyright law provides a whole variety of types of use available to the average user, most notably, the right of "fair use" (Copyright Act of 1976, 2021). It isn't a violation of the copyright holder's exclusive rights if the user can, in good faith, determine that their use is fair. An analysis of four factors determines fair use, based on the intended use:

The purpose and character of the use. Will the user be using the original for commercial purposes or for nonprofit or educational use, as in teaching or making presentations for school assignments? If noncommercial, the use weighs more in favor of fair use.

The nature of the original copyrighted work. Is the work that the user wants to use factual, comprising known facts or data, or is it more creative, like art or creative writings? The more factual the nature of the original, the more the use weighs in favor of fair use.

The amount and substantiality of the original used. Does the amount represent the entire work, a substantial portion, or the heart of the work (without the heart, the rest of the work is less meaningful)? If the amount used is just enough to make the user's point in their new work, it weighs more in favor of fair use.

The market effect of the new use. Will the user's use have any effect on the ability of the copyright holder to make that same use, and will it prevent the rightsholder's ability to monetize that use? If the rightsholder's ability to profit from their work will not be impacted by the new use, the more it weighs in favor of fair use.

Many agreements include a provision for fair use and refer to it. This is good news, but why stop solely at fair use? Copyright law provides several other uses that may be valuable for your organization and its users. For example, Sections 107–122 of the U.S. copyright law permit a wide variety of uses that are helpful to both users and libraries (Copyright Act of 1976, 2021). This includes certain types of reproduction by libraries, compulsory licenses for phonograph records, and musical performances. Some agreements remain silent regarding copyright law. In that case, the licensee can be confident that it and its users should abide by copyright law.

The more odious agreements will enumerate *prohibitions* on the rights granted by law. For example, a licensor may prohibit or limit the number of downloads permitted by a single user in a single session to a precise number. When the user exceeds that number, the licensor gives itself the right to terminate access for that user and even sometimes for the entire organization and all its users. It may also prohibit sharing items with others or displaying or using small portions of content in the users' own works, papers, or presentations, likely fair uses—keep an eye out for such hampering language. In short, while copyright law gives users rights to use others' original works, **the contract may take them away**.

Contract

This part of the document/agreement can really drive the licensee into the weeds. The Uniform Commercial Code (statutory law) governs contracts, which applies to the sale of goods, and common law (judicial precedent and custom) applies to services. License agreements may contain elements of both goods and services. The dominant element (goods or services) and the state in which the licensee is located, determines which law applies. Not only must the licensee and its users comply with the licensed use terms (which govern both permitted and prohibited uses), there are usually additional terms about payment, standards of performance, promises made by both parties, and so on. The contract may require the licensee to perform and promise a wide variety of actions, and consequently, it obligates the licensee to pay large sums of money to rectify any breach of the terms of the agreement (referred to as "damages"). The contractual promises and obligations create liability for both parties but tend to skew risk and liability towards the licensee. The document may include words such as "indemnification," "injunctive relief," "severability," "sanctions," and other equally confounding language that may justifiably intimidate the reviewer. We will discuss what these terms mean a bit further into this chapter.

Following the Law: Other Contractual Promises

An enforceable contract between parties must comprise an offer, acceptance of that offer, and consideration for the offer (usually payment). The license agreement is a contract that includes these elements and should describe a meeting of the minds between the parties. Everyone must have the same understanding of the rights and obligations of each party. Whenever the agreement says that a party "will," "shall," "warrants," or "represents," it means that the party to whom these words refer is obligated by contract law to carry out the subject of the obligation. These contractual terms typically define something the party *should* do or *should not* do. Ideally, both parties are subject to various obligations. For example, the licensor may warrant that it has the right to provide the content to the licensee or promise to make the content available 24x7, ensuring certain levels of accessibility. The licensee agrees to pay on time, offer access only to its authorized community/users, and keep the licensor up to date on authorized IP ranges, among other promises.

Often, the agreement has several business terms that define costs and duration of term, outline the liability of each of the parties and the remedies to make the non-offending party whole. You must scrutinize this language to make certain that your organization can truly comply with the promises made within the agreement. If the obligations are seriously impractical, impossible, or unenforceable, then the licensee must consider changes to the language of the agreement. We will look at some examples in the next section.

ANALYSIS AND REVISION

Reviewing language

It is truly worthwhile to read the agreement in its entirety. The licensor has often hired legal help to draft the agreement, with the intention of protecting it against any negative consequences, even if they are of its own making. It may be your job to read, agree, and/or negotiate these terms. You may have to do this on your own or with a team or other individuals. It is most helpful to develop a supportive relationship with your organization's general counsel's office and/or authorities within your organization with whom you can consult and from whom you can learn about institutional protocol and policy.

Beginning with the licensing uses, know the types of use most required by your organization's authorized user population. Starting with an awareness of what copyright law permits, read the agreement with these needs in mind and look to see if the language prohibits any of the required uses. For example:

- Does an institution require unlimited downloads of material or want to place PDF copies of articles in an e-reserves system? Many licensors prohibit posting PDFs in reserves systems, permitting only links to be shared.
- Does the license permit inclusion of content in electronic course packs? Physical course packs?
- If the content is video or music, does the license allow users to stream to their own electronic devices?

Your users may have needs beyond what the limitations on and exceptions to exclusive rights of copyright holders in the law permit. Ideally, you can change the language to include not only those uses permitted by copyright law but enumerate uses not covered by the law that are necessary for the organization's user population. There are several very good and freely available model license templates from which to draw specific language, as well as my own suggested language (included in Appendix B at the end of this chapter). Liblicense (2014), the California Digital Library (2018), the Library of Congress, and Northeast Research Libraries have produced reputable model licenses from which to harvest language. No need to reinvent the wheel if suitable language already exists.

My favorite clauses that broadly define use in compliance with copyright law are:

Licensee and Authorized Users may make all use of the Licensed Materials as consistent with the United States Copyright Act of 1976 as amended (17 U.S.C. §101 et seq.) including all limitations on and exceptions to the exclusive rights as granted therein.

and

Nothing in this Agreement shall be interpreted to diminish the rights and privileges of the Licensee or Authorized Users with respect to any

of the Licensed Materials, including exceptions to or limitations on the
exclusive rights of copyright owners.

Once the uses made possible by copyright law are included, then move on to include the specific uses tailored to the organization's needs for the specific resource. Some may be general, such as inclusion in course packs, scholarly sharing, usage in course or learning management systems, or interlibrary loan; others will be more specific, such as making archival copies of the entire work, authors' rights, streaming to personal devices, reuse in publications, or text and data mining. The goal here is to include those types of uses that will best meet the needs of the organization's authorized users.

Analyzing Terms of Obligation

Next, we look at the agreement's contractual terms of obligation. A useful exercise is to conduct a word search for those obligating words mentioned earlier: "shall," "will," "represents," and "warrants." You need to be careful of the term "all," as well. Rarely in life can we agree to obligate to *all* of anything, and what may be "all" to one is not "all" to another. For example, referencing "all efforts" is highly subject to individual interpretation.

To what promises or actions do specific terms obligate your organization? Can you comply with them? If your organization is state funded, state law may prohibit you from agreeing to terms such as confidentiality, binding arbitration, or governing law outside of your jurisdiction. Even at private organizations, institutional policy may also prohibit agreeing to certain similar demands.

I mentioned earlier terms that sound confusing and intimidating. Some of these terms may and should raise a red flag as you read through the agreement. They often reference legal obligation and liability, should a party (usually the licensee) fail to comply. Let's scrutinize the following words:

- **Breach**. This refers simply to a party failing to abide by a term of the contract. What happens if one party breaches the terms? Will the license terminate immediately? Is there a period of time the breaching party has to "cure" the breach? What happens to any post-termination rights? Ideally, if the agreement contains post-termination rights, then any termination for breach will only apply to access to content from the date of breach forward, not the material that was available until the date of breach.

- **Changes or modifications**. Don't agree to change the agreement without the signed approval of both parties. Beware of the licensor that requires the licensee to accept changes by virtue of using the content, or language that indicates the licensor may, in its sole discretion, modify the terms at any time (with or without notification or approval of the licensee).

- **Confidentiality or nondisclosure clauses**. Perhaps *some* information needs to be kept confidential, which should apply only to trade secrets or identification of individual users. Some states and institutions prohibit agreeing to confidentiality clauses that reference pricing terms, which is usually the exact thing the licensor hopes to protect and hide from other customers. Your organization/state will dictate how to address confidentiality or nondisclosure clauses.

- **Dispute resolution**. This usually includes mediation and arbitration conducted by a third party. In terms of arbitration, the final decision will be binding on the parties. It is possible that your organization can agree to mediation, but not arbitration. Neither is an inexpensive action. Check with a higher authority at your organization to confirm whether you can agree to either.

- **Governing law, jurisdiction, or venue**. These terms refer to the laws that will apply should a dispute reach the level of a lawsuit. "Governing law" references the laws of the state and country in which the case will be heard. "Jurisdiction" is the proper court to hear the case, and "venue" is the geographical location of the court. Here again, it's wise to check with the higher authority (often, general counsel) at your institution to establish the acceptable protocol. Licensors prefer their own governing law, jurisdiction, and venue. Most organizations (licensees) prefer their own state's governing law, jurisdiction, and venue.

- **Indemnification**. To indemnify is to make the harmed party whole, as if the harm or damage never occurred. Some indemnification is appropriate. For example, a copyright holder may sue the licensee or user even though the licensor granted that use of the content to the licensee, and it was, in fact, used in compliance with the agreement. It is possible that the licensor did not get the needed permissions and should be held responsible and cover expenses of such a suit against the licensee. Many licensors, however, expect the licensee to indemnify them against any prohibited infractions made by its users. Unless the licensee is watching over every single user's shoulder to guarantee they are using the content properly, there is no way that the licensee can agree to this. Indemnification opens the door to a great deal of liability for the organization, so look at this language carefully.

- **Injunctive relief**. This means court-ordered options. An injunction orders the offending party to either *do* or *stop doing* something. It isn't necessarily a bad thing that the language of the agreement includes reference to injunctive relief. We hope that no dispute between the parties will rise to the level of seeking court orders, causing the licensee to hire representative counsel. Instead, the assumption is that the parties will sort out the matter between themselves. Here, as always, the injunctive relief should apply to both parties.

- **Remedies in equity**. Remedies in equity also refer to court-ordered options. They fall into three categories: *specific performance*, requiring a party to fulfill its contractual obligations; *contract rescission*, rendering the contract null and void, unenforceable as though the contract was never executed; or *contract reformation,* clarifying the language/terms of the contract to better reflect the intentions of the parties. We hope that the licensor and licensee will resolve any dispute before it reaches this level. It is worthwhile to be aware of what this reference means and whether any language surrounding these terms needs tweaking.

- **Sanctions**. Sanctions often refer to the licensee doing business with or having any ownership in companies in countries that the U.S. government or its foreign allies have declared subject to sanctions. This rarely comes up. It is more than likely neither party violates authorized sanctions. You might question the licensor why such a clause is in a license agreement and consider deleting if inapplicable to the circumstances.

- **Severability.** Here, if a single section or clause in the agreement is illegal or unenforceable, it does not affect the rest of the agreement. Only that piece will be severed from the whole, and the rest remains intact and enforceable.

- **Waiver.** Many agreements reference a waiver. It refers to the situation where one party breaches or violates the terms of a clause in the agreement, and the non-breaching party does not pursue correction. This does not mean that the non-breaching party has given the offending party a waiver or permission for that breaching activity and its continuation. The non-breaching party *may* pursue a remedy for the breach in the future.

Also consider language that might be deal-breaking for your organization or require you to comply with organizational policy/state law. Some red flags above could be deal-breaking. Others might include language referring to the licensor being granted the right to come physically into the licensee's organization to audit use of the licensed content. Most academic institutions and organizations would prohibit such egregious behavior. Licensors often have the option to monitor anonymous activity remotely, and that should suffice. Depending on your organization's requirements, additional language referencing privacy obligations or opt-out clauses for multiyear licenses may be necessary.

Offering Alternative Language

To create agreements that are a "meeting of the minds," they should be negotiable. Most licensors will agree to some back-and-forth negotiation of the language. Beware of the licensor that says that no other institution has asked for changes, that it does not modify the language that its lawyers drafted, or that it does not have the capacity to negotiate with every single licensee.

Look for language that *expressly* prohibits fair use, certain reproduction activities, performance, display, or modification to the content. If you find language objectionable, change it to accommodate your needs. I suggest using the Track Changes function in Microsoft Word. This way, both you and the licensor will clearly see the changes requested. I also often use the Comment function to add an explanation for the needed change. Remember, if you believe your organization cannot reasonably comply with some terms, then you may say so. For example, you could say "… university/organization/state policy prohibits [the action/promise named] …."

The following are some examples of original clauses and how you might modify them and negotiate using Track Changes. Don't forget to insert a comment to explain why you're making the change, if you think the licensor will need some explanation.

Indemnification

Original:

Except to the extent prohibited by law, Licensee agrees to indemnify, defend, and hold harmless Licensor, its successors, agents, officers, and employees, either in their individual capacities or by reason of their relationship to

Licensor, with respect to any expense, claim, liability, loss or damages including any incidental or consequential damage either direct or indirect, whether alleged, incurred, made or suffered by Licensee or any third party, in connection with, or in any way arising out of the use or disposition of the Licensed Materials by Licensee and its Authorized Users.

Alternative:

*Except to the extent prohibited by law, ~~Licensee~~ **each Party** agrees to indemnify, defend, and hold harmless ~~Licensor~~ **the other Party**, its successors, agents, officers, and employees, either in their individual capacities or by reason of their relationship to ~~Licensor~~ **the Party**, with respect to ~~any expense, claim, liability, loss or damages including any incidental or consequential damage either direct or indirect, whether alleged, incurred, made or~~ **actual damages** suffered by ~~Licensee~~ **the Party** ~~or any third party~~, in connection with, or in any way arising out of ~~the use or disposition of the Licensed Materials by Licensee and its Authorized Users~~ **that Party's negligent breach of its representations and warranties as stated herein**.*

Sample Comment:

The indemnification should apply to both parties, not just the licensor, and refer to actual damages suffered, rather than those that are potential, imaginary, or subjectively perceived.

Many institutions prohibit signing any type of indemnification, and if that is the case at your institution, you must inform the licensor of that. If your institution will accept some liability for its actions or negligence, consider the modification that softens and narrows the liability. Perhaps your organization is only willing or able to accept liability for actual damages rather than anything that happened and could happen. The indemnification should be bilateral, not limited to the licensee indemnifying the licensor only. Also, it is extremely rare that an organization will accept liability for misuse by its users, over whom it has no control. Here, you will want to protect your institution by limiting the scope to only actions taken by the institution and those over whom it presumably does have control, which may include both faculty and staff.

Consider an indemnification that is highly desirable in an agreement:

> *The Licensor shall indemnify and hold Licensee and its Authorized Users harmless for any losses, claims, damages, awards, penalties, or injuries incurred, including reasonable attorney's fees, which arise from any claim by any third party of an alleged infringement of copyright or any other property right arising out of the use of the Licensed Materials by the Licensee or any Authorized User in accordance with the terms of this Agreement. This indemnity shall survive the termination of this agreement. NO LIMITATION OF LIABILITY SET FORTH ELSEWHERE IN THIS AGREEMENT IS APPLICABLE TO THIS INDEMNIFICATION.*

The above clause has the licensor indemnifying the licensee, appropriately, if the licensor has not obtained the licenses or permissions from the creators of the content for its publication and sale. **NOTE**: In many such cases, the licensor requires that it take control over the defense or settlement of the dispute. To permit your institution valuable input into the proceeding, consider the following addition or modification:

> *Provided, however, that Licensee shall have the right to participate at its own expense with respect to any such claim, action, or proceeding and that no such claim, action, or proceeding shall be settled without the prior written consent of Licensee.*

Modification

Original:

Licensor reserves the right to update or modify this Agreement according to changes made to the Service.

Alternative:

Neither party may change or modify this Agreement without the express written permission of the other party.

Sample Comment:

Organizational policy/ state law prohibits licensor from making changes unilaterally to the terms of the agreement.

The licensor is asking for the unilateral right to change the agreement without agreement of the other party. It makes little sense to negotiate an agreement, only to permit one party to make any changes it alone wants later. Beware of the clause that says the changes will go into effect after receipt of notice unless the licensee objects, and in that case, the licensee has the option to terminate. This is unacceptable.

WARNING: An agreement may also refer to terms posted on the vendor's website and may include an option that if the posted terms change, then so does your agreement. This is even more unacceptable. The agreement is the prevailing document, and though the terms posted on the website might be helpful to guide users, they should not be binding upon the organization. Be aware of clauses that reference online terms in the agreement and scrutinize that language for its underlying intent.

Permitted Uses

Original:

Licensee may use the Licensed Materials conforming to Sections 107 and 108 of the Copyright Revision Act 1976 as those provisions have been amended and may be amended from time to time, and conforming to the guidelines developed by the National Commission on New Technological Uses of Copyrighted Works ("CONTU Guidelines"), and in the case of foreign licenses, conforming to the relevant copyright legislation of the Licensee's home country.

Alternative:

Licensee may use the Licensed Materials conforming to Sections 107 and 108 of the Copyright Revision Act 1976 as those provisions have been amended and may be amended from time to time.~~, and conforming to the guidelines developed by the National Commission on New Technological Uses of Copyrighted Works ("CONTU Guidelines"), and in the case of foreign licenses, conforming to the relevant copyright legislation of the Licensee's home country.~~

The fair use and interlibrary loan references are okay, but you may want to include other exceptions and limitations. Consider using a model clause or modify as shown. Reference to CONTU is unnecessary and outdated (from 1974), and CONTU is not law. The latter part, regarding foreign licenses, is okay, but also unnecessary. In general, the user follows the laws of the country in which the user is located.

It is here in the permitted uses section (the license) where you should *add* language that best suits your organization and its users. Consider including clauses that copyright law does not address, such as:

- course and learning management systems
- course packs
- electronic course reserves
- scholarly sharing
- authors' rights (permission for authors of licensed content to reuse their own works)
- streaming
- use in presentations and publications

Assertions and Mitigation

Original:

Licensee and Authorized Users acknowledge and agree that the Licensed Materials are copyright protected and that the sole copyright to the Licensed Materials remains with the Licensor.

Alternative:

*Licensee ~~and Authorized Users~~ acknowledges and agrees that the Licensed Materials are copyright protected and that **as between the parties,** ~~the sole~~ copyright to the Licensed Materials remains with the Licensor.*

Sample Comment:

Users are not party to the agreement, and we do not have authority to agree on their behalf.

Authorized users are not party to the agreement, and the organization does not have permission or authorization from every user to agree to terms on their behalf. The licensee may agree that the materials are copyright protected and that the licensee does not hold the copyright, but can't really know whether the licensor is the sole holder of those rights.

Original:

Licensee shall not permit anyone other than Authorized Users to use the Licensed Materials.

Licensee shall implement security procedures as consistent with best industry standards and authenticate each User initially at logon and intermittently thereafter to ensure only Authorized Users may gain access.

Alternative:

*Licensee shall not **knowingly** permit anyone other than Authorized Users to use the Licensed Materials.*

*Licensee shall implement security procedures as consistent with ~~best industry~~ **reasonable** standards and authenticate each User initially at logon ~~and intermittently thereafter~~ to ensure only Authorized Users may gain access.*

This example mitigates the absolute requirement that access may be given solely to those who are deemed "authorized." I cannot think of a single institution or organization that has absolute control over its users. Of course, the licensee doesn't want to provide access to people who should not have access, and the licensee makes reasonable efforts to limit use via various security and authentication protocols. Can the licensee warrant or promise that some unauthorized person will not gain access? No! Therefore, you must modify the agreement by agreeing that your institution will not *knowingly* take part in providing access to unauthorized persons. I have unofficially polled colleagues about authenticating at login and periodically thereafter and find that it is *not* standard practice to reauthenticate, nor is it feasible to do so. The user is authenticated once they are logged on. Period.

For more information on alternative language, I created a list of go-to clauses to insert where ambiguity, unacceptable language, or prohibitions on activities permitted by copyright law require complete clause overhaul. You can find this language in Appendix B at the end of the chapter. Remember to tailor the terms in these clauses to the tone of the agreement. For example, if the license uses "Subscriber" instead of "Licensee," then you should change the text of the clause to read "Subscriber" instead of "Licensee" when using the suggested alternate clause.

NECESSARY CLAUSES AND CONSTRUCTION

Suppose you're reading an agreement document that is so dense, your eyes roll back up into their sockets. Nevertheless, don't discount the fun, excitement, and challenge of negotiating a license agreement. The agreement may reference some above-noted phrases and terms that I warned you about. That's good, you are on your way. But think whether anything is *missing* from the language in the document. Remember the aforementioned "Offer/Acceptance/Consideration" structure, which makes this a legal agreement. There are terms that must be in an agreement to make it binding on both parties. Ambiguity can be helpful (sometimes), but at times certain terms or elements are a strict requirement. The following are examples of necessary elements:

Parties. Agreements should state who the parties are! This may seem obvious, but I've seen many agreements that skip this. Usually, you find out who the parties are in the agreement's preamble, or at least in the title. It could say something like:

Preamble:

This Agreement is made effective as of [date] by and between [Vendor Name, address] (Licensor) and [Organization name, address] (Licensee).

Or

Title:

License Agreement for [Resource] by/between [Provider name] and [Subscriber entity name]

Subject. It's very helpful to identify the product or resource that is the subject of the license. If it's a series of resources, it may be more generalized. For example, you may be licensing e-books, e-reference works, or e-journals all from the same provider, but identify all the types that will be subject to the terms of *this* agreement.

Dates. Very important! What is the date of the agreement? When does it become effective? Does the date of effect vary from the date of the agreement or from the date of the last party to sign? When does the term end?

Scope or grant. How comprehensive is the agreement, and does it apply to all types of resources offered by the provider? What uses will the grant broadly permit?

Fair use/copyright exception(s). This may not be a "must have" for all organizations, but it's pretty darn important, so don't rule it out. Most educational licensees should require reference at the very least to fair use as a permitted use.

Term. How long is this license in effect? Will it last perpetually or for a single year (12 months from date of signing), or even for multiple years?

Merger clause. This simply states that this agreement is the embodiment of all the understandings between the parties. Anything written or verbally stated outside of the agreement is invalid. Make sure that all uses and terms required by your organization are in the agreement!

Signature lines. This is where the authorized signatories for both parties attest to the validity and mutual understandings of the agreement between the parties.

Consider including other terms that may be critical for your organization in your checklist of necessary language. They may relate to performance of service and availability. Depending on the resource and the likelihood of the vendor changing the platform, consider adding some standards the Licensor should meet before finally executing the change. Accessibility issues are critical in my organization, and we are required to ensure that vendors comply with the WCAG 2.0 (World Wide Web Consortium, 2008) or 2.1 Level AA (World Wide Web Consortium, 2018) standards to make the content accessible by everyone who is an authorized user. (See also some suggested desirable clauses in Appendix B.)

NEGOTIATION

Negotiation is part of the process that brings the parties into agreement on the terms (see more on negotiation in Chapters 9 and 11). Ideally, you have a knowledgeable individual on the licensor side with whom you can have reasonable discussion. This isn't always the case, but no matter; do your best to communicate your organization's needs clearly.

Communication

Communication in person, by phone, email, or video chat should be clear and non-adversarial. **This is not an "us versus them" situation.** Ideally, both parties agree with the terms and can, in good faith, abide by them. This type of communication describes the ever-popular "win-win" situation. Depending on the size of the vendor's company and inclination of the licensor, you may hear such phrases as:

No other institution/organization has asked for changes ...

or

There are too many customers to make a different agreement with each ...

Understand that negotiation takes time away from selling the product and may involve additional staff and expense on the side of the licensor to negotiate an equitable agreement. Of course, you are also spending time and effort, and are presumably being paid to negotiate terms that best meet the needs of your institution. The vendor may say you can take it or leave it. And where there are objectionable terms, I recommend you leave it. Not the easiest decision, but it happens from time to time. You may have to explain to a requesting user why you cannot accommodate the acquisition.

If you don't appear to the licensor as someone who is open to honest discussion, the road to successful negotiation is all the harder. Again, this isn't supposed to be adversarial. Most disagreement arises over either permitted types of use or demanded acceptance of unreasonable liability based on impossible or unachievable promises to do or not do something. You can only agree to that over which your institution has control. Anything else is a deal-breaker. Be friendly; both parties are working towards a common goal. The licensee wants to buy, and the licensor wants to sell. It may be useful to understand the other party's negotiation style and appeal to it. Does the person prefer verbal or written communication? How does the person frame their questions or responses? Work to create a side-by-side feeling; both parties are working to solve a common issue.

A frequent problem with some negotiations is that the person with whom you are working on the licensor's side isn't an individual who has authority to approve changes. This adds to the time it takes to complete negotiations. Where possible, try to work directly with those who have authority to change the agreement, and get your communications in writing. Phone or video calls are fine, but follow up that kind of communication with a written summary of your discussion so you can refer to your verbal agreement. Send a copy of the summary to the other party as well, so you are both working from the same understanding.

Addenda Versus Amendments

NOTE: Addenda add things to an existing document, and amendments change the text of the existing document. It is good to understand the distinction between the two. Many use the two terms interchangeably, but they represent different types of modifications to an agreement. They both append to the original and are considered as one with the original.

In some interactions, a licensor may be unwilling to change the text of its standard agreement but is willing to create an amendment to its template. This is very nearly the same as negotiating and changing the original text. An amendment should point directly to the clause(s) to which the changes or replacements are being made. My standard amendment template references the parties, the specific licenses, and date of the original agreement. Then it says that "From the Date hereof the License Agreement shall amend the following: …" Here, reference to specific clauses, subclauses, and paragraphs should show how you will write them, such as:

*The original text of Section 8(A)(i) shall be deleted and replaced with ...
[add the new text].*

Alternatively, the text might say:

*The original text of Section 8(A)(i) shall be revised to read...[insert
changes made to the original language].*

Sometimes the original language is fine but is lacking or missing elements
that you believe would better meet the needs of your organization. Here,
you need an addendum to add to the original agreement. My template addendum looks very similar to my template amendment, stating parties and
date of the original agreement, but says instead, "From the Date hereof the
License Agreement shall add and include the following: ..." The reviewer
then enumerates whatever it is they want to add. It may be as simple as
adding a new product or a type of use, such as text/data mining.

ALTERNATIVES AND NON-LICENSES

Model licenses

License agreements need not always be fraught with anxiety and where
possible, there is no need to reinvent the wheel. As I mentioned earlier, there are many freely available and reliable model licenses from
which to choose. You can harvest these for specific language that you
tailor to your institutional needs and the tone of the license provided
by the vendor. Sometimes, you can use the model instead of the licensor's original. Some licensors haven't hired expensive lawyers and don't
have a standard license, and you can offer one instead. You can create your own organizational model license based on one of these freely
available models.

SERU

SERU: A Shared E-Resource Understanding (National Information Standards Organization, 2015) is a NISO Recommended Practice and something that you may use in certain circumstances instead of a formal license agreement. To be effective, both parties must be in the SERU registry (National Information Standards Organization, n.d.). SERU is an expression between licensors and licensees of a practical set of understandings about the use and provision of the licensed materials. At my institution, to help with invoicing and resource tracking, we created a template SERU document, a single page stating the standard language of SERU:

SERU STATEMENT OF AGREEMENT between [XXXX UNIVERSITY] and [VENDOR/PUBLISHER]

Date:_____

The parties named herein have mutually agreed, in the absence of a separate license agreement, to follow the Shared Electronic Resource Understanding (SERU) as published at the NISO SERU website (http://www.niso.org/committees/SERU/) for the acquisition and use of the following resource(s):

[We insert the resources subject to the understanding (as below), list names/contact of both parties, include a statement affirming registration with SERU, dates of document/dates of subscription term(s)/ perpetual access for resources, and NO signature lines.]

Resource Title	Term	Price	[other]

The parties by entry of contact name and affiliation acknowledge this understanding and affirm that they have registered with SERU (https://sites.google.com/niso.org/registry-seru/):

[XXXX UNIVERSITY]	[VENDOR/PUBLISHER]
Contact Name: Address: Email Address/Phone Number: Date:	Contact Name: Address: Email Address/Phone Number: Date:

Both parties get a copy for their records.

SERU isn't appropriate to use for all types of acquisitions but may be worth considering as long as the resource and intended uses aren't overly complex. A close review of the SERU Recommended Practice (National Information Standards Organization, 2015) is worthwhile, to familiarize yourself with the elements pertaining to acquisition, authorized users, and use of the materials. As noted above, as is the practice at my institution, create a document noting the specifics that are unique to the resource(s) subject to SERU. For example, whether it is subscription or perpetual access or has archival rights. You can add these elements into the text of the description as needed.

CONCLUSION

Frankly, you would need an entire book rather than a single chapter on licensing to cover all the agreements, situations, and scenarios for an ever-increasing number of types of e-resources and yet still lack every possible instance. I don't mean this chapter to be a comprehensive covering of the entire landscape of licensing e-resources for libraries. I provide some suggestions for further reading below.

The environment for e-resources is ever changing, but there are some standards, legal and practical, that aren't subject to drastic evolution.

Monitoring copyright law is extremely helpful, as is being aware of your organization's policies and requirements.

Additionally, you must assure that the license and its obligating terms are possible to accommodate within your organization. Completing and executing the license doesn't mean that you just file it away and are done with it. You must work closely with your e-resources colleagues to make certain that the reasonable efforts that you have agreed to make will comport with what they can carry out. Further consultation with your IT department may also be necessary, for the same reason. Much of this will depend on how your organization is constructed for compliance with its protocols and policies. You may also have to consult with selectors or other constituent members of your organization to guarantee that invoicing and payments get into the pipeline. Consider, too, how best to inform your user population about appropriate use of the licensed materials and whether additional security measures need be undertaken.

FINAL WORDS

You thought we'd never get here, right? Nevertheless, I have a few last words to impart. I always felt that part of my job was to ensure that someone or some entity did not sue the library over an agreement that the library made with a provider. A key to reducing/mitigating litigation means that you must know your organization's policies and requirements, your users' intended use, and the level of risk your organization will accept. This will vary from organization to organization. The license should protect both parties and hold both parties to reasonable promises and expectations. The key is not to promise that over which you have no control, and to negotiate the broadest and most likely terms of use. Then control what you can, by working organizationally to exercise those reasonable efforts to inform your user population about appropriate use. When made aware by the licensor of a breach in use, take the opportunity to educate not only the infringing user but review organizational policy to inform more appropriately. It's always a work in progress, but these tips should help give you confidence to create a viable and less risky agreement. Good luck and happy licensing!

CITATIONS AND FURTHER READING

California Digital Library. (2018). *Standard license agreement* [public version]. https://cdlib.org/wp-content/uploads/2019/02/CDL_Model_License_2018.05.14 _public.docx

Copyright Act of 1976, 17 U.S.C. §101 *et seq.* (2021). https://www.copyright.gov/title17 /title17.pdf

Halaychik, C. S., & Reagan, B. (2018). *Licensing electronic resources in academic libraries.* Chandos.

Harris, L. E. (2018). *Licensing digital content: A practical guide for librarians* (3rd ed.). ALA Editions.

Liblicense. (2014). *Liblicense model license agreement with commentary.* http://liblicense .crl.edu/wp-content/uploads/2015/05/modellicensenew2014revmay2015.pdf

Library of Congress. *Terms and conditions for license of electronic resources.* https://www.loc .gov/acq/devpol/lc-model-license.pdf

Lipinski, T. A. (2013). *The librarian's legal companion for licensing information resources and services.* ALA Neal-Schuman.

NERL. *Northeast Research Libraries Consortium generic license agreement for electronic resources.* http://nerl.org/wp-content/uploads/2019/06/ NERLModelLicense-061019.pdf

National Information Standards Organization. (n.d.). *NISO SERU registry.* https://sites .google.com/niso.org/registry-seru/

National Information Standards Organization. (2015). *SERU: A shared e-resource understanding.* https://www.niso.org/standards-committees/seru

U.S. Const. art. I, § 8. https://constitution.congress.gov/browse/article-1/section-8/

World Wide Web Consortium. (2008). *Web content accessibility guidelines (WCAG) 2.0.* https://www.w3.org/TR/WCAG20/

World Wide Web Consortium. (2018). *Web content accessibility guidelines (WCAG) 2.1.* https://www.w3.org/TR/WCAG21/

APPENDIX A: LICENSE REVIEWER CHECKLIST

Use the following as a checklist when reviewing agreements. These terms and clauses are ones where problematic issues may arise. Pay close attention to the language the licensor presents in these sections.

License/Agreement/Terms and Conditions/ Subscription Agreement

The naming of the document may change, but where the document includes terms and conditions, that is a license agreement or contract for all intents and purposes. The agreement means licensee and its users have license to use the content in the manner described by the terms and conditions stated.

Red-Flag Terms

- all
- best
- represents or warrants
- shall or will
- is obliged/obligated
- responsible

Red-Flag Clauses

- **Breach.** What happens if one or the other party breaches the terms? Does the license terminate? Is there a cure period? What happens to our rights to materials post-termination?
- **Changes or modifications.** No changes should be made to the agreement without the signed approval of both parties.
- **Online terms**. Reference to terms posted on the licensor's website affecting the negotiated license.
- **Confidentiality or privacy**. Some confidential information should be kept so, some not—how to distinguish between the two? Statute may prohibit state institutions from agreeing to confidentiality clauses. What does the licensor want to keep private? Does the privacy clause protect privacy of the licensee's users?

- **Conditioning access**. Where the users have to create a profile or account before they can gain access to the content. Do not collect and use this data for marketing purposes.
- **Dispute resolution**. Depending on your local authority, you might be able to agree to mediation, but not arbitration. Others may agree to both or neither.
- **Governing law/jurisdiction/venue**. Our library can agree to [home state] or [general counsel–approved alternative state] in the United States. Occasionally, for international entities, depending on general counsel's advice, the U.K. may be used, but preference is generally for the United States. Check with your authority on foreign jurisdictions.
- **Indemnification**. Be careful! It is appropriate for the licensor to indemnify the licensee for claims that arise due to infringement of intellectual property rights of an individual when the licensee and its users use the materials in compliance with terms of the agreement. *NEVER indemnify the licensor for the acts or misdeeds of the licensee's users* (over whom the licensee has no control).

Deal-breakers

- **Arbitration.** It may be preferable to go to court rather than be subject to arbitration to settle a dispute. You should check with your institution's general counsel or another institutional authority.
- **Audits.** Some vendors want to come onto the premises to look through the licensee's records to ensure that use of the materials is in compliance with the terms. Many organizations don't permit on-site audits. The licensor can remotely monitor usage.
- **Indemnification.** Under no circumstances can the licensor be indemnified for anything over which the licensee does not have control (e.g., its authorized users). A caveat is that the licensee presumably

has control over staff and employees, as the licensee's agents. (Contact general counsel or authority for clarification.)

- **Unilateral modification.** The parties have gone to the trouble of negotiating an agreement; there is no way that any party can or should make changes, but licensors still insert this from time to time.

Must-haves (All agreements should contain these elements)

- **The parties.** Usually, the preamble names the parties to the license.
- **Subject of the license.** What are you licensing? A single journal, or will it apply to all journals?
- **Scope and grant of the license.** How can you make use of the materials, and what are the boundaries?
- **Fair use exception.** At a minimum, you should get reference to fair use in there.
- **Interlibrary loan (ILL).** You want this for most things, but it may not be available for databases or whole e-books.
- **Term.** Length of time the license is in effect.
- **Merger clause.** What this license embodies is what the parties are meant to have. Any other promises or obligations written or spoken outside of this agreement are invalid.
- **Modifications/amendments.** Any changes must be agreed on between the parties and signed off on.
- **Signature lines.** In most cases, it is the signatures required for both parties, especially if it is a merger clause.
- **Dates.** Very important! You need to know when things will happen.

Highly Desired (Organizational needs will dictate this list, adding or subtracting where required)

- **Accessibility.** Our library's preference is level AA criteria of the WCAG 2.0 guidelines (minimum). *NOTE:* Some institutions may require this.
- <u>All</u> limitations and exceptions in U.S. copyright law. [PREFERRED]
- **Archival/backup copies.** For perpetual access or dark archiving.
- **Authors' rights.** Best with journals/books and databases.
- **Branding.**
- **Course pack usage.**
- **Downloading and printing copies of material.**
- **E-reserves usage.**
- **Learning/course management systems, such as Canvas.**
- **Opt-out clauses.** For multiyear agreements, to be triggered due to financial constraints.
- **Perpetual access accommodation.** Because we aren't buying print, we want some assurance that we'll have access post-cancellation. LOCKSS, CLOCKSS, and Portico options are good. If access is solely via the licensor platform, it may cost a lot, in which case we'd like to negotiate an alternative to getting all the files for our own access and storage.
- **Privacy.** User information must be kept private. Where the licensor or platform provider requires users to create accounts or profiles, it may not sell or use that data for marketing purposes. Only anonymous user data may be collected for user statistics.
- **Reuse in publications/presentations.** (Probably a fair use, but it doesn't hurt to name it.)
- **Scholarly sharing.** To support collaboration between colleagues, in insubstantial amounts.
- **Text/data** mining.

APPENDIX B: SUGGESTED CLAUSES FOR E-RESOURCE LICENSES

This section includes language that you can plug into an agreement if the existing language is objectionable, insufficient, or absent, but possibly required by the organization for inclusion. You should make changes to elements of this language consistent with the existing language of the original agreement (e.g., if the original uses "Subscriber" instead of "Licensee").

Clauses

Accessibility	Governing Law	Platform Migrations
Added Rights	Indemnification	Termination
Advertisements	Jurisdiction	Text/Data Mining
Authors' Rights	Notice	User Data Collection
Branding	Opt-Out Clause	Transparency
Fair Use		Warranties

Accessibility

Licensor shall provide Licensed Materials in compliance with the Level AA criteria of the Web Content Accessibilities Guidelines (WCAG) 2.0, as published by the World Wide Web Consortium's Web Accessibility Initiative (http://www.w3.org/WAI/WCAG20/quickref/).

If vendor is neither compliant nor willing to become compliant (a last resort, if no agreement to ADA or VPAT):

Licensor shall explore and take reasonable steps to provide Licensed Materials in compliance with the Level AA criteria of the Web Content Accessibilities Guidelines (WCAG) 2.0, as published by the World Wide Web Consortium's

Web Accessibility Initiative, in a timely manner. Where Licensor is unable or unwilling to become compliant, the Licensor shall indemnify and hold Licensee harmless for any losses, claims, damages, awards, penalties, or injuries incurred, including reasonable attorney's fees, which arise from any claim by any third party or Authorized User of an alleged infringement of such compliance with regard to Licensor's provision of Licensed Materials. Licensor shall have the sole right to defend such claims at its own expense. NO LIMITATION OF LIABILITY SET FORTH ELSEWHERE IN THIS AGREEMENT IS APPLICABLE TO THIS INDEMNIFICATION.

Compliance with Section 508 of the Rehabilitation Act of 1973 (as amended):

Licensor shall comply with and provide Licensee with a copy of Licensor's completed Voluntary Product Accessibility Template *(VPAT) form, which follows Section 508 (29* U.S.C. 794d*) standards, as applied to the Licensed Materials.*

*URLs:

- *Voluntary Product Accessibility Template (VPAT)*: https://www.section508.gov/sell/vpat/
- 29 U.S.C. 794d: https://www.govinfo.gov/content/pkg/USCODE-2011-title29/pdf/USCODE-2011-title29-chap16-subchapV-sec794d.pdf

Added Use Rights

Rights not covered under the U.S. Copyright Act within a limitation or exception.

Authors' Rights *(see below)*

Course and Learning Management Systems

Licensee and Authorized Users may make limited digital copies of Licensed Materials for posting to a closed, specific course or learning management system that is accessible only by registered course participants for teaching and learning purposes.

Course Packs

Licensee and Authorized Users may use a reasonable portion of the Licensed Materials in preparing course packs or other educational materials.

Course Reserves (Print and Electronic)

Licensee and Authorized Users may use a reasonable portion of the Licensed Materials in connection with specific courses of instruction offered by Licensee and/or its parent institution.

Scholarly Sharing

Authorized Users may transmit to a third-party colleague, in hard copy or electronically, minimal, insubstantial amounts of the Licensed Materials for personal use or scholarly, educational, or scientific research or professional use but in no case for resale. In addition, Authorized Users have the right to use, with appropriate credit, figures, tables, and brief excerpts from the Licensed Materials in the Authorized Users' own scientific, scholarly, and educational works.

Advertisements

Licensor shall not place advertising on website pages or services on which the Licensed Materials covered under this Agreement are made avail-

able. To avoid doubt, this restriction does not include advertising that is part of the content itself, such as ads found within journals, magazines, archival, or primary source material.

AUTHORS' RIGHTS

Example 1—Most like the Association of Research Libraries (ARL) definition:

Authors' Rights to Use Their Own Work. *Notwithstanding any terms or conditions to the contrary in any author agreement between Authors and Licensor, Authors affiliated with Licensee whose work ("Content") is accepted for publication within the Licensed Materials shall retain the non-exclusive, irrevocable, royalty-free right to use their Content for scholarly and educational purposes, including self-archiving or depositing the Content in institutional, subject-based, national, or other open repositories or archives (including the Author's own web pages or departmental servers), and to comply with all grant or institutional requirements associated with the Content.*

For the avoidance of doubt, it is the intent of the parties to this agreement that Authors are third-party beneficiaries of this provision of the Agreement.

Definitions:

Content*. Any version (except for the PDF version formatted in the publisher's layout and bearing the publisher's trademark) of any work by an author affiliated with the Licensee that is published in the Licensed Materials.*

Scholarly and educational purposes*. Purposes encompassing teaching, research, and institutional needs, including but not limited to the right to (a) use, reproduce, distribute, perform, and display the Content in con-*

nection with teaching, conference presentations, and lectures; (b) fully use the Content in future research and publications; (c) republish, update, or revise the Content in whole or in part for later publication; (d) meet requirements and conditions of research grants or publishing subventions provided by government agencies or nonprofit foundations; and (e) grant to the Author's employing institution some or all of the foregoing rights, and permission to use the Content in connection with administrative activities such as accreditation, mandated reports to state or federal governments, and similar purposes. In all cases, the Author and/or the Author's employing institution will be expected to provide proper citation to the published version.

Repositories or archives. *Open-access digital repository services, such as those provided by the Author's employing institution, an academic consortium, a discipline-based entity, or a governmental funding agency, provided that the archived version is not the PDF version formatted with the publisher's layout and trademark.*

Example 2:

Authors' Rights to Use Their Own Work. *Notwithstanding any terms or conditions to the contrary in any author agreement between Authors and Licensor, Authors whose works are created while in the employment of a Participating Member Institution and supported by such Participating Member Institution, and whose submitted version of their work ("Content") is accepted for publication within the Licensed Materials, shall retain the non-exclusive, irrevocable, royalty-free right to use their submitted version of their work ("Content") for scholarly and educational purposes, including self-archiving or depositing the Content in their respective Participating Member Institution's institutional, subject-based, national, or other open repository or archive (including the author's own web pages or departmental* *servers), and to comply with all grant or institutional requirements associated with the Content.*

To avoid doubt, it is the intent of the parties to this agreement that Authors are third-party beneficiaries of this provision of the Agreement.

Definitions:

Content. *The submitted version ("Content") of a work by an author affiliated with Licensee that is published in the Licensed Materials.*

Scholarly and educational purposes. *Purposes encompassing teaching, research, and institutional needs, including but not limited to the right to (a) use, reproduce, distribute, perform, and display the Content in connection with teaching, conference presentations, and lectures; (b) fully use the Content in future research and publications with proper attribution; (c) republish, update, or revise the Content in whole or in part for later publication with proper attribution; (d) meet requirements and conditions of research grants or publishing subventions provided by government agencies or nonprofit foundations; and (e) grant to the Author's employing institution permission to use the Author's submitted version of their work in connection with administrative activities such as accreditation, mandated reports to state or federal governments, and similar purposes. In all cases, the Author and/or the Author's employing institution will be expected to provide proper attribution and citation to the published version.*

Repositories or archives. *Open-access digital repository services such as those provided by the Author's employing institution, an academic consortium, a discipline-based entity, or a governmental funding agency.*

Example 3:

An author affiliated with the Licensee whose work is accepted for publication within the Licensed Materials may self-archive an author-created version of their article on their own website and or in their institutional repository. They may also deposit this version on their funder's website or funder's designated repository at the funder's request or as a result of a legal obligation, provided it is not made publicly available until 12 months after official publication. They may not use the publisher's PDF version, which is posted at www.publisher.com, for the purpose of self-archiving or deposit. Furthermore, the author may only post their version provided acknowledgement is given to the original source of publication and a link is inserted to the published article on the publisher's website. The link must be accompanied by the following text: "The final publication is available at www.publisher.com."

BRANDING

To clarify that the content and services subject to this Agreement are made available to Authorized Users by Licensee, Licensor will provide Licensee the option to brand the Licensor's platform in a format equal or greater in prominence to Licensor's own marks, with the name of Licensee, including text, logos, or other branding marks at Licensee's discretion.

FAIR USE (AUTHORIZED USE)

Licensee and Authorized Users may make all use of the Licensed Materials as consistent with the United States Copyright Act of 1976 as amended (17 U.S.C. §101, et seq.), including all limitations on and exceptions to the exclusive rights as granted therein.

Nothing in this Agreement shall be interpreted to diminish the rights and privileges of the Licensee or Authorized Users with respect to any of the Licensed Materials, including exceptions to or limitations on the exclusive rights of copyright owners.

Governing Law

This License shall be governed by and construed in accordance with state of X State law; the parties agree that any dispute arising out of or in connection with this License will be subject to and within the jurisdiction of the courts of X State.

Notes:

1. If you are at a private institution, check with your general counsel's office; otherwise, probably the state in which your institution is located will be preferred. For publicly funded institutions, most states mandate that the governing law must be in the state in which the institution is located.
2. Many institutions cannot accept arbitration clauses but may accept mediation. Check with your general counsel's office.

INDEMNIFICATION

Each party shall indemnify and hold the other harmless for any losses, claims, damages, awards, penalties, or injuries incurred, including reasonable attorney's fees, which arise from any alleged breach of such indemnifying party's representations and warranties made under this Agreement, provided that the indemnifying party is promptly notified of any such claims.

Note: Under no circumstances can an institution indemnify the licensor for misdeeds of its authorized users. (See also Warranties.) You can only indemnify the licensor for what you represent and warrant within the agreement (as long as you don't represent or warrant anything over which you have no control).

Preferred:

The Licensor shall indemnify and hold Licensee and Authorized Users harmless for any losses, claims, damages, awards, penalties, or injuries incurred, including reasonable attorney's fees, which arise from any claim by any third party of an alleged infringement of copyright or any other property right arising out of the use of the Licensed Materials by the Licensee or any Authorized User in accordance with the terms of this Agreement. This indemnity shall survive the termination of this agreement. NO LIMITATION OF LIABILITY SET FORTH ELSEWHERE IN THIS AGREEMENT IS APPLICABLE TO THIS INDEMNIFICATION.

Note: Where the licensor will indemnify licensee (your institution is the indemnified party), many will also put in something to the effect that it indemnifies the licensee so long as it can **take control over the defense or settlement** of the dispute. Your institution may not want to give up that control and should replace that kind of language with:

Provided, however, that X Institution (or Licensee) shall have the right to participate at its own expense with respect to any such claim, action, or proceeding and that no such claim, action, or proceeding shall be settled without the prior written consent of X Institution (Licensee).

JURISDICTION

As noted with Governing Law, jurisdiction/venue should be in the same state (or county of the state) as Governing Law.

NOTICE

After the U.S. addresses for "regular" notices, add:

> *Any legal notices or other legal documents provided to Licensor as provided above shall constitute valid legal service, and Licensor expressly waives any further service of process otherwise required under the Hague Convention.*

(Or, you can put in whatever international convention you think you might be pulled into.)

OPT-OUT CLAUSE

Version 1:

> *Licensor acknowledges that the ability of Licensee to participate in the Agreement is subject to and contingent upon the availability of funds appropriated by the institutional budget processes. Licensee shall make good faith efforts to obtain the funding to meet its obligations as set forth in this Agreement. Licensee may terminate its participation in this Agreement only at the start of a subscription term (i.e., January 1) by giving Licensor notification in writing no less than sixty (60) (or 30) days prior to the start of that subscription calendar year.*

Version 2:

> *Licensee reserves the right to terminate this Agreement within thirty*

(30) days of release of its budget for fiscal period (July 1, 20XX–June 30, 20XX) or for succeeding years, to the extent concurrent with the term of hereof, if such budget results in a loss of substantially all of the financial support from which Subscriber intended to satisfy its payment obligations hereunder, provided that (i) such termination is motivated by Licensee's good faith belief that its budgetary allotment for university library acquisitions is insufficient to satisfy Licensee's obligations hereunder; and (ii) alternative sources of funding are not reasonably available or expected to become available at the time Licensee's payment obligation attaches. In such circumstances, this Agreement will terminate as of the end of the calendar subscription year for which Licensee had paid in full the License Fee and all other fees and charges due under this Agreement.

PLATFORM MIGRATIONS

Licensor shall give notice to the Licensee that content will be moving to a new platform no less than sixty (60) days before the migration commences. The Licensor will provide the Licensee with a migration timeline and, where possible, a preview environment. Licensor shall use reasonable efforts to provide continuous service throughout any platform migrations, ensuring that Licensee does not lose access to content.

TERMINATION

If the vendor terminates due to breach and the licensee couldn't cure it, the licensee should secure maintenance of its perpetual access rights (where applicable) to the content to which the licensee had access before the date of the breach. The language on this will vary depending on the type of resource.

Upon termination for cause, Licensor shall provide Licensee with either per-
petual online access to the Licensed Materials that were available up to the
date of the breach or, in the alternative, a copy of Licensed Materials acces-
sible up to date of breach in machine-readable, mutually acceptable format.
Post-termination use shall be subject to the terms of this Agreement.

TEXT/DATA MINING

Old, but still good:

Authorized Users may use the licensed material to perform and engage
in text mining/data mining activities for legitimate academic research
and other educational purposes.

Update—Places burden on provider to give us the raw data (where possible, on a cost recovery basis or at no extra charge):

Licensor shall provide, either online at its website, through a third-party
service (such as LOCKSS, CLOCKSS, or Portico), or to Licensee one full
copy of the Licensed Materials in raw data format. The raw data may be
used by Authorized Users to perform text and/or data mining functions
and algorithms for legitimate academic research and other educational
purposes in accordance with the terms of this Agreement.

Liblicense version:

Authorized Users may use the Licensed Materials to perform and en-
gage in text and/or data mining activities for academic research, schol-
arship, and other educational purposes; utilize and share the results of
text and/or data mining in their scholarly work; and make the results
available for use by others, so long as the purpose is not to create a

product for use by third parties that would substitute for the Licensed Materials. Licensor will cooperate with Licensee and Authorized Users as reasonably necessary in making the Licensed Materials available in a manner and form most useful to the Authorized User. If Licensee or Authorized Users request the Licensor to deliver or otherwise prepare copies of the Licensed Materials for text and data mining purposes, any fees charged by Licensor shall be solely for preparing and delivering such copies on a time and materials basis.

CDL version:

Authorized Users may use the Licensed Materials to perform and engage in text and/or data mining activities for academic research, scholarship, and other educational purposes and may utilize and share the results of text and/or data mining in their scholarly work and make the results available for use by others, so long as the purpose is not to create a product for use by third parties that would substitute for the Licensed Materials. Licensor will, upon receipt of written request, cooperate with Licensee and Authorized Users as reasonably necessary in making the Licensed Materials available in a manner and form most useful to the Authorized User. Licensor shall provide to Licensee, upon request, copies of the Licensed Materials for text and data mining purposes without any extra fees.

USER DATA COLLECTION TRANSPARENCY

Licensor may require users to create accounts or profiles to take advantage of personalized features of the Subscribed Products. Licensor shall, in addition to linked associated terms of service and privacy language, provide a short, clear, and obvious statement at the location of the user click-through acceptance that references how users' data is collected and the purposes of its use made by Licensor. Users are not required to create accounts or profiles to make all use the Subscribed Content, including all features, except for those that are personalized.

WARRANTIES

Typically, vendors don't provide any warranty; the product comes "as is." However, they should have the requisite authority and right to license the content to us.

Licensor warrants that it has the right to license the rights granted under this Agreement to use Licensed Materials, that it has obtained any and all necessary permissions from third parties to license the Licensed Materials, and that use of the Licensed Materials by Authorized Users in accordance with the terms of this Agreement shall not infringe the copyright of any third party.

Be careful about what you represent and warrant in the license. Generally, the licensee can warrant that it has the authority to enter into the agreement and represent that it will use **reasonable efforts** to do one thing or another (e.g., inform authorized users that they must or must not use the materials in a certain fashion). If asked to indemnify the licensor, perhaps limit indemnification only for grossly negligent breach of the licensee's representations and warranties in the license. Make sure you don't represent or warrant for anything over which your institution does not have control. (See also Indemnification.)

Five

Implementing Access

Allyson Rodriguez and Athena Hoeppner

Congratulations! You have now spent a lot of money—money that isn't your own. So that the money is well spent, you must set up the resource so users can find it, use it, and know its purpose. Implementing access to a resource encompasses three areas:

- access
- administration
- marketing

One must consider each of these areas with each new e-resource and evaluate the applicability of each step in each situation. To set up access, you must understand what the resource is, find the correct access point or points, and test all forms of access. Correct administrative setup needs careful attention, because it will affect access and later parts of the e-resources management cycle. Finally, users must know that a resource is available and understand how to use it. Finding the right balance of time, effort, and promotion or advertisement isn't always an easy task, but all require attention!

ACCESS

Access Points

Libraries typically manage multiple access points to help users discover their online offerings. The library catalog, database pages, discovery service, and subject guides are widely used by libraries, and course pages in learning management systems like Canvas or Blackboard are common access points to e-resources in academic settings. RSS feeds, online newsletters, and social media posts also serve as access points when a new resource is announced, though they are typically not intended to be maintained as long-term access points. To select the appropriate access points for a given resource and purpose, you must consider what the resource is and what level of linking is best for the content. Is it a single database with one link? Is it a collection of e-books with hundreds of MARC records with links in the record's 856 field? Is it a set of archival collections, in which each collection has a distinct landing page?

Quite often, libraries will use the catalog for journal, book, video, and other title-level links. The database list is most often used for links to top-level platforms, such as to EBSCOhost or ProQuest; to specific databases or collections on the platform, such as Academic Search Premier or ABI Inform; or to top-level publisher sites, such as SpringerLink. Discovery services and link resolvers offer deep links to articles, chapters, and other content. Subject pages, course pages, newsletters, and RSS feeds may have a mixture of top-level links, database links, and deep links to articles and chapters. You will likely use a combination of the available access points for resources, with different link levels and different purposes in mind.

For each access point and resource, consider whether it is better for your users to land on a simple search page, an advanced search page, an informational page, or somewhere else. If the vendor supplied a link that lands on a page other than the one you prefer, and you are unable to determine a stable URL for the preferred page, reach out to the vendor and

Figure 5.1
Example Access Points and Link Levels

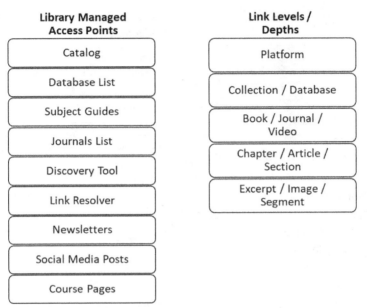

Library Managed Access Points	Link Levels / Depths
Catalog	Platform
Database List	Collection / Database
Subject Guides	Book / Journal / Video
Journals List	Chapter / Article / Section
Discovery Tool	Excerpt / Image / Segment
Link Resolver	
Newsletters	
Social Media Posts	
Course Pages	

request a stable URL of the page that is best for your users. If you believe it is best to have multiple links to different landing points for a resource, find or request stable URLs for each page you need. Check the functionality of each new URL you receive: Does it work and resolve as expected, or does it return an error? This initial work up front enables your users to have appropriate access to the newly acquired e-resource.

Whichever access point you use, you must check that the links you intend to use 1) work without error, 2) are where you want your users to land, and 3) work with your preferred authentication method(s). Some access points, such as the library catalog, discovery services, and LibGuides pages, are specifically intended to host and manage links. They offer tools that help with authentication, offer readable and persistent URLs, and provide link checkers. Discovery services and link resolvers will maintain article-, chapter-, and title-level URLs in their

Figure 5.2
Typical Linking Choices for Each Type of Access Point

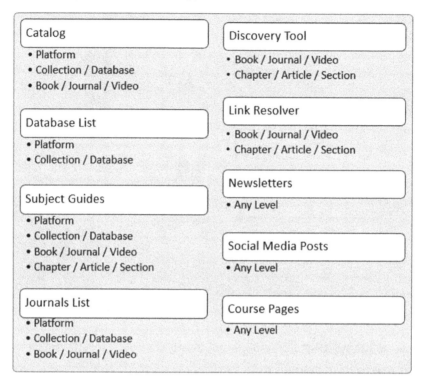

knowledgebases. Other access points, such as course pages and social media posts, don't include such helpful tools, and managing the links on
these access points proves especially difficult. Frequently, these sorts of
links are created by faculty, subject librarians, the library's communication and marketing staff (if applicable), and other people who aren't
e-resources management staff and aren't as versed in the nuances of linking. Provide guidance to library staff and faculty on finding persistent
URLs and creating links that will authenticate.

A vendor may provide MARC records for e-resources as part of the
acquisition or for an additional fee. If MARC records are available, first
determine if they are freely available from the vendor or if there is a cost

associated with these records. Records may also be available from different sources, including ERMS providers (e.g., ProQuest, EBSCO, or OCLC). Prior to acquiring records—free or paid—it is important to understand what kind of edits will be required to load and maintain the records. For example, will vendor-provided records include your institution's proxy prefix with the access URL?

It is important to work closely with the cataloging and metadata staff in your library to determine the best method for acquiring and adding MARC records as access points. Then, work with the vendor to determine the best place to find and download these files and share the file locations and credentials necessary to retrieve the records with colleagues loading the records.

If the vendor updates MARC records, or if it adds to or removes content from the e-resource, note the frequency of these updates and how, when, and where the updates will be made available. If the vendor does not update records as needed, users may miss content, encounter dead links, or see inaccurate information. Once files are downloaded, it is essential to verify the access point is working; check several record URLs to make sure that they work.

Authentication and Authorization

As you are creating links to use in the access points, you need to know how the vendor will recognize and authorize connections from your users. The contract language typically spells out who is considered an authorized user and may lay out the acceptable forms of authentication. Be sure to know the contract terms well enough to comply with all requirements as you set up authentication options. For example, if only on-site users are authorized, then reporting your on-site IP range to the vendor, or even a username and password controlled by the service desk, may be sufficient. However, if remote access is permitted, then a proxy server, SAML, VPN, or other method of authentication is needed to provide access to the largest allowed audience. (For more about negotiating authentication and authorization of e-resources, see Chapter 4).

When you enable access to e-resources, you will see a variety of options for supporting authentication and authorization. Most libraries use at least two approaches to authentication, with IP authentication and EZproxy being the clear frontrunners. Some specialized databases may require you to assign usernames and passwords to every user each semester, some may require that you share the database link only on course pages where students have already logged in via the learning management system (referring URL), and others may require federated authentication to pass pseudonymous attributes about the person logging in.

Some sample approaches to authenticating users and authorizing access:

- **IP authentication**: Give the vendor the IP addresses for your library or campus. Any connection from within that IP range is authorized for access. It is the basis for both on-site, proxy server, and VPN access. A section below gives more details about IP and proxy server authentication.

- **Federated authentication using Security Assertion Markup Language (SAML)**: Use a trusted identity provider (IdP) to verify the identity of a person and pass along assertations about the person so the database/service provider can determine whether the person is authorized to access the content or service. OpenAthens and Shibboleth are the most widely used federated authentication services in North America. A section below gives more details about federated authentication.

- **Usernames and passwords and personal user accounts**: Login credentials can be managed entirely by the library, with a limited number available for all potential users, or individuals may be able to create their own accounts after some verification that they are authorized to access the resource, usually by being on-site.

- **User ID or ID pattern match**: Upload the full list of user IDs to the vendor site or establish a connection so the vendor can check user files on the fly, or enter some string that is present in all valid user IDs.
- **Referring URL**: Give the vendor a URL for a page or site that can only be reached by authorized users, such as a course page in a learning management system.
- **Google CASA; OAuth**: Associate a person's library affiliation and authorized status with Google or other non-library accounts and allow access based on the Google (or other) account login.

Whichever solutions your library chooses, as an e-resources manager you will need at least a basic understanding of the common authentication services and a good working relationship with all parties involved in administering them for your library.

IP Authentication

To set up IP authentication, libraries give the content vendor the IP addresses used at their institution, and the vendor configures their services to authorize access for requests coming from the approved IPs. Typically, large institutions like colleges and libraries have a stable range of IP addresses, and the networking and information technology staff can tell you the IP range or list. The IP range is generally associated with the physical location, and the assumption is that anyone able to access the network and computers at that location is authorized to access the online content.

Often, the order form or license agreement has a section for listing the IP addresses to be used for authentication. You may be able to enter the IP range in the administrative interface, if the vendor offers one. Additionally, libraries can opt to enter their IP ranges in the IP Registry (https://theipregistry.org), and the IP Registry in turn distributes the set of IPs to participating vendors.

Below are some typical approaches to entering/displaying IP ranges. Follow the directions from each vendor when entering your IPs:

123.145.6.78 – 23.145.6.100
23.145.6.78/100
123.145.*.*
123.145.000.000 – 123.145.255.255

IP authentication is the basis for some other approaches to providing off-site access, including VPN (virtual private network), Google CASA (campus-activated subscriber access), and proxy server. A VPN can allow off-site users to establish a secure connection to the institution's network, and then tunnel all internet traffic through that connection. The vendor sees the traffic coming from the institution's network, with the institution's IP, so it authorizes the user to access subscribed content. Usually, VPN servers and settings are controlled by institutional IT staff, and not all VPNs are configured to allow access to remote sites, such as library databases.

Google CASA authentication relies on agreements between Google and the content vendors. When a person uses their phone or computer to sign in to Google Scholar while on campus, Google sets a token that associates that device with the college or university. When the person uses the device to access content from a vendor that participates in Google CASA, they are recognized as associated with the college or university and are authorized to access the library's subscribed content. The tokens last for a month and are automatically refreshed when the device is used on campus. Google CASA does not involve any setup by the library beyond reporting the IP ranges to the vendors, as described earlier.

Proxy Server/EZproxy Authentication

Proxy servers work by mediating connections between a browser and a content site. When a person logs in to a proxy, the proxy server rewrites URLs on webpages to incorporate the proxy domain. All traffic for the changed links goes first to the proxy server, which requests the page from the target site. Vendor sites see the proxied request coming from the proxy server's IP. If it recognizes the IP as associated with a subscribing library, the vendor site returns the requested page to the proxy, the proxy server once again rewrites the link URLs, and then delivers the page to the browser. OCLC's *About EZproxy* page provides a clear, basic introduction (https://help.oclc.org/Library_Management/EZproxy/Get_started/About_EZproxy).

EZproxy, created by Chris Zagar in 1999, has served libraries and their users as the most used method for providing off-site access for decades. Its functionality, sophistication, and complexity have grown since its creation, and it was purchased by OCLC in 2008. Customers can host an EZproxy server locally or can use an OCLC hosted version with greater support from OCLC for setting up and maintaining the necessary configurations. The rest of this section is based on EZproxy, though some portions may also apply to other proxy services.

Major steps for e-resource access management using EZproxy:
A star (☆) indicates the task is very likely to be done by e-resources management staff.

Set up and configure an EZproxy server and authentication method

If your library hosts its own EZproxy server, then your systems personnel will most likely set up and administer the server and core configuration files that set the session length, specify how

users authenticate to start a session, establish security certifi-
cates, and other technical settings. If your library uses OCLC's
hosted EZproxy, OCLC will administer these core settings. In either case, be prepared to offer input and to test the settings. If
you are responsible for the settings, refer to OCLC's EZproxy
documentation.

Configure various settings and web pages used by the proxy server

In-depth instructions on configuring a proxy server are beyond
the scope of this chapter. Frequently, systems personnel handle
the more technical aspects of administering the proxy server. If
you are the proxy server administrator, consult the documentation provided by your proxy service for guidance.

☆ Configure targets and stanzas

An EZproxy stanza is a set of instructions that control which
sites to proxy and how to handle the site content and features.
For example, a library will want the proxy to work for subscription sites like SpringerLink and JSTOR but will not want the
proxy to bother handling connections to sites that aren't part
of the library's online collection, such as Facebook. The content
vendor might give you the correct stanza to use as part a subscription activation email. If not, OCLC maintains a list of stanzas
(https://help.oclc.org/Library_Management/EZproxy/Database
_stanzas/000_Database_stanzas_recent).

If neither the vendor nor OCLC have the needed stanza, you
may be able to create a simple working stanza following the instructions from OCLC's *Introduction to Database Stanza Directives*

(https://help.oclc.org/Library_Management/EZproxy/EZproxy
_configuration/Introduction_to_database_stanza_directives).

☆ Report your proxy server IP to vendors

Be sure to include your proxy server IP address when you report
your IP addresses to vendors. If your institution hosts the proxy
server on site, it likely has an IP within your default IP range.
If you use a hosted service, such as OCLC's hosted EZproxy or
OpenAthens proxy, the proxy IP may be very different from your
network IP range.

☆ Create starting-point URLs to use in your access points

Starting-point URLs (SPUs) initiate a proxy connection to a service. They combine a proxy stem with the URL for the target
site or page. For example: *https://login.proxy.youlibrary.edu
/login?url=https://somedatabase.vendor.com*

SPUs may include additional segments to specify authentication
method and other settings, and the target URL can be a site-level
link, like in the example above, or a deep link to an article or seg-
ment on a site. For deep links, the target URL may need to be
encoded to preserve punctuation. Be sure to test SPUs before using them in your access points.

Note: Once the EZproxy connection is established, the rewritten
links and the URLs in the browser address bar take a different
form than the SPU. For example: *https://somedatabase.vendor
.com.proxy.youlibrary.edu/....* The best practice is to use the SPU
form of linking as access points, not the rewritten version.

E-resources management staff often manage at least the stanza files for EZproxy and may administer the other configurations. Maintaining EZproxy connections in working order has become complicated, as internet security, site functionality, and the sheer number of websites all morph and expand. Fortunately, EZproxy has an active, knowledgeable community base that you can turn to for help (EZPROXY-L@OCLCLISTS.ORG), and good, basic documentation is available from OCLC.

Federated Authentication (e.g., OpenAthens, Shibboleth)

With federated authentication, user authentication and provision of access are distinct processes. The user authenticates by sending their login credentials to an IdP controlled by the college, library, or other organization that the person is affiliated with. The IdP then asserts to the service provider that the person is, or is not, a member of the organization and may provide additional attributes about the person. The service provider determines whether to grant access to the person based on the assertations and attributes. It is possible for a person to successfully authenticate but be forbidden access to the requested service or content. For example, if a library licenses content for the College of Medicine, a student in Computer Science will be able to authenticate via the university's IdP, but the database provider will not let the student access the content because they don't have the attribute stating they are a College of Medicine student. The OpenAthens video *How It Works* provides an easy-to-understand, simplified illustration of federated authentication (https://www.openathens.net/providers/federation/).

As with EZproxy, you can create URLs to initiate a session and connect to a service, a process described in more detail later in this section. Once the session is started, a browser cookie is set that contains the information needed to maintain the session and to support single sign-on into other services and vendor sites. While the session cookie is active, the person will not need to reenter login credentials to reauthenticate. Unlike EZproxy, federated authentication does not mediate the connection or rewrite URLs. After the connection is established, traffic flows directly between the end user's browser and the service provider's site.

Federated authentication is newer and more technically involved to implement than IP and proxy-based authentication. Additionally, to use federated authentication the library must belong to a federation and must have an IdP that can send assertations about attributes to a service provider using SAML encoding. As a result, fewer libraries use federated authentication than rely solely on IP and EZproxy. However, its popularity and importance have grown rapidly since 2019, and many large publishers favor it for security and for potential user account personalization. Even if your library does not currently use federated authentication, your organization may already be using it for some purposes, and you are likely to encounter it as an option in library systems and vendor administration pages.

Here is a brief glossary of federated authentication terms:

Federation: In this context, a federation is an organization of member institutions including colleges, universities, libraries, publishers and content providers, and other Service Providers. The members agree on technology and standards to use and agree to accept assertations from the IdPs used by the member. In short, it establishes trust and protocols to enable authentication and authorization. In the United States, colleges and universities may be members of the InCommon Federation, which uses Shibboleth, and libraries of all types may contract to be included in the OpenAthens Federation. There are dozens of federations worldwide.

Identity provider (IdP): A system that has information about a group of people affiliated with an organization, with unique IDs for every user and typically other details. Examples of IdPs include

LDAP (Lightweight Directory Access Protocol), ADFS (Active Directory Federation Services), and Azure AD. Organization IT staff usually control the IdP options.

Service Provider (SP): In the context of SAML, a system that offers content or services. For libraries, common Service Providers include database, journal, and book platforms. Colleges and universities often have systems that are service providers, such as the learning management system, the registration system, and other services that students and employees need to access and that require secure logins.

EntityID: The unique identifier for a federation member. For library authentication purposes, you will tell Service Providers your federation and your entityID so they know how to connect to your IdP. Example entityID: https://idp.university.edu /openathens. For OpenAthens, you will have a numeric organization ID as well as the entityID.

Attributes: Information about a person and their role within the organization, such as department and email address. The organization controlling the IdP decides which attributes it is willing to share with each service provider.

Assertations: A set of SAML encode statements about the person requesting access to a service, to be delivered from the IdP to the service provider. It can include several attributes or a simple statement that the person is a valid member of the IdP's organization.

Security Assertion Markup Language (SAML): A standard for encoding assertations and communicating between IdPs and Service Providers (SPs).

Single sign-on (SSO): When logging in to one service allows you to access other services. Federated authentication can potentially provide SSO across all the services in the federation. For example, a person could sign using OpenAthens to access a Wiley article, then go to Gale to search a database without needing to re-enter login credentials. SSO can be achieved by federated authentication but isn't exclusive to this approach.

Where are you from (WAYF): Many vendors, especially journal publishers, have a sign in button on their sites with an option to login through a user's institution or federation. The sign in process guides users through identifying the authentication option for their institution, usually by asking the user to pick their federation (which is confusing to many people) or to type the name of their institution. The service then directs the person to the correct login form. After successful authentication, the person is returned to the vendor's site. The WAYF login service lets people authenticate without having to hunt for a library-provided starting-point URL.

SeamlessAccess: SeamlessAccess is an effort to improve the user experience for the federated identity-based authentication offered on vendor sites. As mentioned in the WAYF description, the login process on vendor sites can be confusing. Publishers who opt to participate in SeamlessAccess will use an icon for their login button with the SeamlessAccess logo. The WAYF process will allow people to find their institution by its name, common nicknames, or by email address domain. Once the person logs in, SeamlessAccess will remember their institutional affiliation. The next time the person uses a SeamlessAccess login, even if the person is on a different vendor's site, the service will suggest the affiliated organization.

Major Steps to Use Federated Authentication

A star (☆) indicates the task is very likely to be done by e-resources management staff.

Join a federation

If you work in an academic setting, your institution may already be a member of InCommon and may have Shibboleth for federated authentication to services. Typically, institutional identity management and information technology units administer the settings, with a focus on campus and enterprise needs more so than library authentication. Libraries can contract to join the OpenAthens Federation, either directly or through a service partner. OpenAthens has several partners that will assist with setup and support, listed on the OpenAthens Partners page (https://www.openathens.net/our-partners/).

Set up an IdP

Typically, configuring the IdP is done by identity management and IT units as part of joining a federation. Your organization may already have an IdP used to authenticate people for access to various services, such as online courses, library user accounts, and so on, and you may have more than one IdP available. Which IdP is used may affect the attributes that are available for authorization and personalization by services.

Set attribute release policies

Your IdP likely has more data about people affiliated with your organization than is needed for access to library subscriptions.

The IdP controls which attributes it generally sends to Service Providers, and the specific attributes to be released to specific Service Providers. In most cases, the service provider needs only to know that the person connecting is a member of your organization in good standing. Some services require more attributes. Library staff can promote user privacy by encouraging selective release of attributes. REFEDS (Research and Education FEDerations) offers guidance on attribute mapping and release policies that protect privacy, and the EduPerson and EduPersonAffiliation specifications are especially helpful for library purposes (https://wiki.refeds.org/display/STAN/eduPerson).

☆ Enable specific Service Providers

Just as EZproxy uses the target stanzas to control which sites it will handle, federated authentication involves explicitly enabling services that can use the authentication. Enabling a service involves an administrator setting up the specifics of which attributes will be sent, sending your federation and entityID to the service provider, testing the connection, and troubleshooting issues. For Shibboleth, the identity management unit is likely responsible for these steps. Contact the Shibboleth administrators whenever you need to enable a new service.

OpenAthens does much of the legwork for libraries, so enabling a new service can be as simple as finding the service in the OpenAthens Resources Catalog, clicking the "enable" button, and telling the service provider your OpenAthens entityID. Some vendors have sections on their library administrator pages for entering your entityID and other federated authentication details.

☆ Test connections and access

Test the connections by using the vendor's WAYF login and by creating a link (described below). Check that all the pages and features maintain the authorized state and work correctly. If you released attributes for a specific purpose, be sure that the intended purpose works and has the data it needs.

☆ Create links that will start a session

There are two styles of URLs to connect to services using federated authentication.

Shibbolized or Athenized URLS: You can construct URLs that include elements to specify the federation, the entityID for your organization, the server that will process the request, and the destination URL. These URLs can be long and complex, and you will need guidance about exactly what to include for each service provider.

Example of a Shibbolized or Athenized URL structure: https://federation-sp.vendor.com/session/init?entityID={entity}&shib-return-uri={target}&subcode=abc

OpenAthens redirector URLs: OpenAthens redirector URLs are similar to EZproxy starting-point URLs. The first part of the link is the OpenAthens server and a string to identify the library. The second part is the service to connect to after authentication.

Example of an OpenAthens URL: https://go.openathens.net/redirector/college.edu?url=https://vendor.site.com/

OpenAthens redirector URLs have the advantage of being far simpler and easier to construct on the fly. Behind the scenes, OpenAthens converts the simple URL into the correctly constructed Athenized URL to connect to the service. However, the redirector service does not handle all connections perfectly. In some cases, you may need to use the Athenized URL.

Enabling Authentication in Access Points

Once you have your authentication service in place, you can apply it to access points. One approach is to add authentication links to access points one at a time. A more efficient approach is to configure the main access points to apply the proxy stem across the board and then make exceptions if a specific resource needs a different approach to authentication. LibGuides, many integrated library systems, e-resources management systems, discovery services, and link resolvers allow you to enter your preferred proxy or authentication stem centrally so that the authentication stem is added to all e-resource links at the point of access. This approach can save a great deal of time if you need to change your authentication stem for any reason.

Testing Access

Now that you have URLs in place, it's time to check your work. Understanding your library's systems and setup will go a long way toward figuring out where any errors or breakdowns are occurring. Check access to all e-resources systematically to verify functionality. Obviously, you can never check every situation that users will experience, but by hitting the big ones, you can head off many problems. This means checking on-site and off-site access, checking each location type with each commonly used browser, and checking access on computers and both Android and iOS mobile devices. This is a lot of work; however, it can provide you with invaluable information and give you a chance to head off problems before they surface for users. For example, if you know that a resource isn't optimized for a certain browser or device you can add a note to the resource warning users of this. Not all users will notice or heed this warning, but those who do will have a less frustrating experience accessing the resource.

One additional note: To test access off site, use a VPN so that your computer has an off-campus IP address or go off site yourself. If off-site access isn't working, check the proxy stanza for accuracy, review the URL and make sure both the proxy prefix and the URL are accurate, check multiple browsers to make sure it's not a browser-specific issue, and try clearing the cache on your browser in case previous cookies are blocking access. Additionally, check access in different browsers and check access using browsers' incognito modes, which will void existing cookies. If issues persist, you may need to reach out to the proxy server administrator, the vendor, or both to figure out the problem.

When testing access and troubleshooting access problems, it's important to understand that each library has a different set of systems that interact in uniqueways.

ADMINISTRATION

Whether the resource is from a vendor or platform that is new or well known, you may have to set up an administrative portal. Often an administrative portal will provide information on current holdings, usage statistics, MARC records, contact information, or other information users don't need access to. If the resource is on a platform or through a vendor that you already have an established relationship with, all you'll need to do is confirm and record that the usage statistics, holdings data, and/or MARC records for the new resource are available through its administrative portal. Storing administrative access information in the same place and same format each time allows colleagues and successors to find the relevant information quickly and easily. Often, libraries use an e-resources management system (ERMS) to track and document information related to each resource. This could include administrative information like administrative login information, where and how usage statistics are available, invoicing records, holdings information, support, and sales contacts.

If the platform or vendor is new, you may have to create an account. Verify how or where to create the account with the vendor and create the account early in the process; there could be information valuable to the setup of a resource in that portal. When setting up the account, it's best practice to use a shared inbox or generic email address in case you leave the organization. This will allow your successor to maintain access to the information they need. It's also essential to record the login information for the administrative portal, for the same reason. Some libraries record admin site information in a shared document, in an ERMS, or in some other way. How or where you record the information isn't as important as that it's recorded in an accessible place. Finally, test the portal to guarantee links are functioning, the information in the portal is correct, and you can find all of the information you need.

If there is no administrative portal to set up, work with the vendor so that it has the appropriate contact information in case of technical issues, invoicing, or payment problems, and for providing usage statistics, if they are available. You should also make sure that you have the appropriate contact for each of these issues as well as where to find any necessary records, documentation, or other information.

MARKETING

The Plan

Once your resource is set up and properly tested, it's time to tell the world, or at least your users, about it. How much marketing or promoting you do, what types of marketing, and the targets of your advertising efforts should all be considered carefully with each resource. Some resources may require less marketing or a more focused approach, and you should consider that when planning your promotion efforts. For example, a resource with a niche focus, such as crystalline structures of inorganic materials, may need a small amount of promotion to a small, focused group, since they will be the main users and already know about the resource. However, using a variety of marketing methods for a large interdisciplinary database from a well-known platform would benefit the e-resource's large user group. An interdisciplinary database from a new platform would require a wide array of marketing methods to share in-depth information with the variety of potential users.

A promotion plan may be a useful tool to help you bring together your ideas into a cohesive strategy. The plan can be as simple as a document outlining the goal or goals of these promotion efforts; users who would find the resource beneficial; the timing of the promotion or advertising; and the methods, resources, or tools that you intend to use. This can also be a great place to document an interesting fact, useful feature, or strange quirk about the resource. Providing this information up front can draw users to access the resource or provide them with helpful tips to have an easier experience when initially accessing the resource.

The Methods

As you create your plan for marketing, consider a variety of methods for reaching your intended audience. An email briefly explaining how to access the resource, a unique or interesting item within the resource, and links to training materials or guides to use the resource can be a quick, easy, and cheap way to reach a large group of potential users. However, mass emails can sometimes be offputting to those receiving them and may go unread if not sent properly or if sent too frequently. It's best to send mass emails only when the appeal of the resource is wide and a library representative can send the email from an address the reader will recognize. If email isn't the best option, but electronic communication is preferred, using social media outlets is another way to show off new acquisitions. Social media content should be quick to read and easy to digest, so keep posts brief and exciting. Physical advertisements such as flyers, posters, or digital signage can be especially useful when your library has heavy foot traffic or when email isn't appropriate. Again, these should call attention to major features, interesting facts, and, most importantly, how to access the resource easily. Do not include a lengthy URL, but instead provide brief instructions on how to find the resource in the library catalog or create and provide a shortened URL. For marketing purposes, some shortened URL services provide click-through statistics that can help libraries determine which of their marketing materials are most effective. Finally, don't forget about in-person opportunities to promote a new library resource. This could come in the form of one-on-one conversations with users, or through more formal presentations or training sessions. Remember, vendors often offer training sessions, which can allow users to ask in-depth questions and get the experts' answers. Make any helpful training documents or online tutorials available to users, whether created by library staff or vendors.

The Timing

As you consider how to market, to whom, and how much to advertise e-resources, it's also important to consider when you will launch the promotion plan. Consider the natural patterns of library use and plan accordingly. For example, in an academic library, summers are often very slow, with most of the students and faculty away from campus; summer would not be a good time to advertise the launch of new library resources. In public libraries, summers are often very busy, with parents bringing in children more often and otherwise increased foot traffic; summer would be an excellent time to promote a new e-resource geared toward children.

When considering timing, you will also want to consider the amount of time you want or are able to put into promoting a new resource. Do you want to make a big splash with a lot of advertising, in-person promoting, and an event? Or would it make more sense to have a minimalistic approach, with only a brief email? You will want to consider things such as your workload, the range of appeal of the resource, the cost of the resource, and the likelihood of a user finding and understanding how to use the resource.

SKILLS NEEDED FOR IMPLEMENTING ACCESS

Communication

Communication is essential to setting up access to e-resources. From communicating on technical aspects with content providers and internal stakeholders to communicating about features, uses, and access with users, it's essential that technical services staff can communicate in writing and orally while tailoring those communications to each audience they encounter. Library staff must be able to communicate effectively in a variety of formats to a wide array of constituents. (See more in Chapter 9.)

Synthesizing Information

Taking complex information from a variety of sources and making that information usable for various stakeholders is crucial to the e-resource acquisitions process. It's no less important than implementing access to the resource. Setting up a resource successfully requires combining information from the vendor or content provider and from internal library stakeholders, such as the proxy server administrator, to create a complete picture of the access requirements. Additionally, taking the complex information regarding a resource and compiling it into an understandable set of promotional materials allows users to get the best picture of a resource.

Collaboration

With so many people involved, including the proxy server administrator, catalogers, content providers, subject specialists, frontline staff, and more, library staff implementing access to e-resources must be willing, ready, and able to collaborate with many colleagues. Failing to collaborate with any area can mean the failure of your resource to launch or can lead to a lack of use. Additionally, by building collaborative partnerships with each of these stakeholders, you can often find creative solutions to problems and provide better service to library users.

Flexibility

Often, setting up access to a new resource will not go as planned. A content provider will have part of an IP range incorrect, there will be a typo in the proxy stanza, the URL will land on a page that does not make sense to you, your promotional efforts will not hit the mark, or any other of a million possible problems will occur. Taking each issue in stride, finding a workaround or fix, and understanding the root of the error will help prevent issues moving forward, but each of these responses requires flexibility. With e-resources, it's important to remember that just because something should work or should happen doesn't mean that it will—be flexible.

Creativity

While it's easy to recognize the need for creativity when considering the promotional efforts around an e-resource, creativity is also important in setting up the access to the resource. Whether you're determining what the best landing page is or testing access for the variety of ways users connect to e-resources, creativity is vital.

CONCLUSION

Properly implementing access to e-resources can mean the difference between a user seamlessly accessing content they need and becoming frustrated and moving on to a different resource, or abandoning their search altogether. Setting up and testing access, accurately setting up administrative information and recording that information, and marketing e-resources are essential to the lifecycle of the e-resource.

Accomplishing and keeping track of all of this can be burdensome; however, clear documentation can help. Appendix A provides a brief checklist to track the process. Be sure to modify the checklist to meet the needs of your individual institution and individual resources. Not every step is necessary for each resource or each institution. To accomplish these tasks, library staff must use excellent communication with both internal and external stakeholders, synthesize complex information for a variety of audiences, collaborate with colleagues inside and outside the library, be flexible as things change, and creatively tackle any issues that arise. When access is properly implemented, resources can be used and evaluated effectively, leading to a more relevant library collection.

CITATIONS AND FURTHER READING

Bunton, G. A. (2017). EZProxy: The key to remote access. *The Serials Librarian, 73*(2), 119–26. https://doi.org/10.1080/0361526X.2017.1338635

Bunton provides a quick introduction to the basics of what EZProxy is and how it works, and tips on how to implement and maintain the system. The author starts with a brief introduction about the necessity for off-site user authentication and a brief history of EZProxy. Bunton then explains the simplified version of setting up EZProxy and administration of the server. Finally, Bunton explains system directives, with examples included, as well as a brief section on configuring user authentication. This article prepares the novice user of proxy servers.

Carter, S., & Traill, S. (2017). Essential skills and knowledge for troubleshooting e-resources access issues in a web-scale discovery environment. *Journal of Electronic Resources Librarianship, 29*(1), 1–15. https://doi.org/10.1080/1941126X.2017 .1270096

Carter and Traill discuss both the need for troubleshooting e-resources and the increasing complexity of this process with the introduction of new technologies, such as web-scale discovery services. Even though the maintenance and troubleshooting of e-resources are widely considered major issues with e-resources, there are still problems with the tracking, workflows, and training of staff involved in troubleshooting. The meat of the article includes essential knowledge and skills for troubleshooting, common points of failure and how to identify those points, and methods for training library staff on troubleshooting and documenting this work. While the authors recognize that each library environment is different, they provide generalized concepts that are applicable to many systems and environments.

Chisare, C., Fagan, J. C., Gaines, D., & Trocchia, M. (2017). Selecting link resolver and knowledge base software: Implications of interoperability. *Journal of Electronic Resources Librarianship, 29*(2), 93–106. https://doi.org/10.1080/1941126X.2017.1304765

This article begins with a clear and concise explanation of what a link resolver is and why it's important for end users. The authors provide a brief history of the link resolver as well as specifics for their institution. A lengthy literature review provides context for the evaluation completed by the authors. While the nature of the article is somewhat technical, the authors explain the evaluation criteria and the implications in terms that most library staff will understand.

Dubicki, E. (2008). Basic marketing and promotion concepts. *The Serials Librarian.* 53(3), 5–15. https://doi.org/10.1300/J123v53n03_02

In this article, the author notes the importance of marketing library resources and acknowledges that those undertaking marketing activities are often not trained or prepared for that work. With understandable definitions and a clear breakdown of what a marketing plan could entail for library staff, the author provides a basis for promoting library resources and briefly explains specific methods of marketing.

Erlandson, R. J., & Erb, R. A. (2013). *Technology for small and one-person libraries: A LITA guide.* Chicago: ALA TechSource.

This book focuses on staff with limited experience managing technology who work at small and one-person libraries serving small populations. Three sections, each with multiple chapters, provide basic information on library technology basics, e-resources, and the virtual library. While the content targets small libraries, other library staff who are new to managing e-resources will find the content easy to understand and, with practical information, very useful. Erlandson and Erb provide helpful additional readings at the end of each chapter.

Kennedy, M. R., & LaGuardia, C. (2013). *Marketing your library's electronic resources: A how-to-do-it manual for librarians.* Chicago: Neal-Schuman.

Kennedy and LaGuardia use this book to guide libraries through the process of creating a marketing plan, implementing that plan, and then evaluating it. For each portion of the marketing plan, the authors provide real examples from public and academic libraries, giving readers a chance to learn from other libraries. This book offers excellent background material for further research. Even those without a background in marketing or who are unfamiliar with the terms and concepts will be able to use this book to create, implement, and assess a marketing plan to drive usage of e-resources.

APPENDIX A: IMPLEMENTING ACCESS CHECKLIST

Access		
	Resource record complete in ERMS, spreadsheet, database, etc.	
	Correct/appropriate URL	
		URL tested
		On-site access tested
		Off-site access tested
	Vendor has correct IP ranges	
	Proxy server is updated to include stanza of new resource	
	MARC records downloaded	
		MARC record links tested
	Link resolver set up	
Administration		
	Administrative portal	
		Set up
		Tested
		Login information recorded
	Usage statistics (may be same as administrative portal)	
		Location found
		Login information recorded
	Branding sent to vendor	
Marketing		
	Marketing plan created	
		Emails
		Physical advertisements (flyers, posters, digital signage, etc.)
		Interesting/unique facts and features noted
		In-person promotion opportunities
		Social media promotion

		Training and documentation
		Vendor-provided or internal
		Made available (posted, link, blog, sent to individuals, meetings scheduled, etc.)

Six

Maintaining E-Resources in Core Library Systems

Athena Hoeppner

Electronic resources require maintenance and troubleshooting throughout the year to keep holdings accurate, subscriptions current, and links updated. Platform migrations, content evolution, technology or policy updates, and myriad other changes occur, sometimes with pre-planning and communication, and sometimes unplanned and with no forewarning. Changes to e-resources and to the core library systems may take place without a hitch if they are well planned, communicated, and coordinated. Unplanned changes are likely to introduce problems and interrupt access. A combination of proactive maintenance and nimble responses to unplanned changes and problems are necessary to create reliable access.

This chapter discusses e-resources maintenance in the context of services and systems used to discover and access the library's online collections. It starts with broader concepts, including an overview of core library systems and their administrative backends, good e-resources maintenance habits, and proactive maintenance versus reactive troubleshooting.

Mid-chapter, the focus switches to more specific situations and content types, and maintenance considerations. The chapter does not provide specific procedures for maintenance. Rather, it presents information and observations that e-resources management staff can apply when they develop their own procedures for their specific systems and content.

CORE LIBRARY SYSTEMS AND E-RESOURCES MAINTENANCE

E-resources staff strive to make library technology work so users can find and access the library's online collection. No matter how many hours we spend immersed in title spreadsheets, in the guts of a link resolver, or redlining indemnification clauses out of licenses, the true focus of our work is connecting people with content. We collaborate with others to develop and maintain a set of user-facing tools for discovery and access that can provide a successful user journey from the library homepage, through discovery tools, authentication, and, ultimately, access to the full content of relevant material.

Figure 6.1 illustrates a simplified journey for a user seeking full text. The user starts from a library-created site, such as the library homepage, database list, or the library catalog. They navigate to a database or discovery service, which provides citations to full text. The citation metadata is fed via OpenURL to the link resolver, which presents links to the full text on a publisher's platform. The links are routed through a user login as needed for authentication into subscription databases and full text. This over-simplified illustration shows user-facing systems and services typically managed, in whole or in part, by the library. The larger information ecosystem includes many more elements, and the user's journey may start in a learning management system, with a web search, or with a link in an email, and may bypass many of the library's systems. For the sake of simplifying discussion, I refer to groups of systems in the diagram as *core library systems* for the rest of the chapter.

Each core library system has an administrative module or backend system where library staff maintain their holdings information, create the linkages between the systems, enable authentication for off-site access, add logos and branding, and otherwise manage the e-resources and technologies (see Figure 6.2). The work of enabling access and maintaining e-resources is ongoing and happens in these modules, often as a collaborative effort between the e-resources staff, catalogers, web developers, vendors, and systems employees.

Figure 6.1
Idealized Diagram of a User Interacting with Core Library Systems

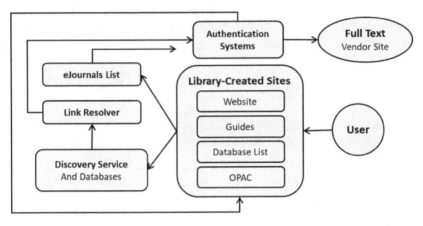

Figure 6.2
Diagram of Admin and Backend Modules for Core Library Systems and Linkages Between the Systems

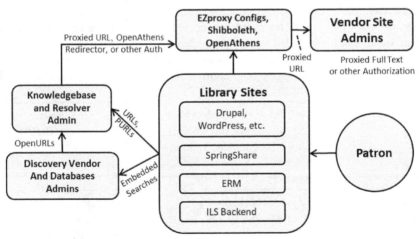

Figure 6.3
Library Systems and Administration

System or Service	Likely Admin Modules or Systems	Likely Managed By
Library Website	WordPress, Drupal, or other site-creation and hosting service	Library Staff; Web Designer; Library Systems
Research Guides	SpringShare's LibGuides, or other site-creation and hosting service	Library Staff; Web Designer; Public Services
Library Catalog	Integrated Library System (ILS)	Library Systems; Catalogers; Acquisitions; Other Departments; Consortia
Discovery Service and Databases	Vendor's discovery administration websites	Vendor; E-Resources Management Staff
Database List	LibGuides database assets, ERMS, or other list creation and hosting service	E-Resources Management Staff
Online Journals and Books List	Link resolver knowledgebase and title list service (e.g., EBSCO Admin and Holdings and Link Management, Summon 360) or ERMS	Vendor; E-Resources Management Staff
Link Resolver	Link resolver knowledgebase (e.g., EBSCO Admin and Holdings and Link Management, Summon 360, ExLibris SFX, OCLC Link Resolver)	Vendor; E-Resources Management Staff
Authentication Systems	EZproxy, Shibboleth, OpenAthens, WAM	Institutional IT; Authentication Service Provider; E-Resources Management Staff

Database and Journal Vendor Sites	Each platform may have its own admin and statistics site	Vendor; E-Resources Management Staff

Of course, core library systems are only a fraction of a larger information ecosystem. Library users interact with outside systems, networks, and devices that outside units control in part or whole. A significant responsibility of e-resources management staff is to understand the user's journey through the information ecosystem and the connections between library and external systems. We can leverage hyperlinks, embedded forms, widgets, and APIs to create the connections to enable a good user journey.

Once the connections are created, much of the work of maintaining and refining those connections fall to e-resources management staff. Therefore, it's imperative that you:

- Familiarize yourself with how the systems are connected in your setting.
- Find out which options and settings you can control.
- Look for opportunities to make core library systems work smoothly with the other systems in your setting (e.g., integration and interoperability with the learning management system, or achieving single sign-on (SSO) so authentication carries over from system to system).
- Create and maintain consistent navigation, link labels, headers, and branding, combined with SSO, to generate a cohesive user experience that is easier to maintain.
- Develop working relationships and channels to communicate with the owners of the systems, so you know whom to contact and how to contact them to communicate changes and for assistance with troubleshooting.

E-RESOURCE MAINTENANCE HABITS

While e-resources management staff will need to work in many different systems to maintain many different resource and service types, you can generally apply some good habits and approaches to make maintenance more consistent and efficient.

Get Information and Help from Others

E-resource content and systems are the result of collaborations and agreements between two or more parties, such as the library and a content vendor; the library and the IT department; or the library, a content vendor, and a platform vendor. The other parties can often provide you with information, help maintain accurate records of and links to the online content, and help you troubleshoot problems.

You can request information, such as a spreadsheet with titles and ISSNs for a licensed package, seek help with troubleshooting (e.g., identifying and resolving failed authentications when using OpenAthens). Often, the active involvement of all parties is required to resolve an issue. Don't hesitate to contact your customer service representative, consortium helpline, service provider technical support, or IT and networking support. Keep track of individual names and email addresses of people you can contact, as well as the general support email address and phone numbers, so you can contact the other parties as needed. It is often most effective to include a known individual and the general support contact in emails when you report problems.

You can also seek help from within your library, especially from acquisitions and cataloging, but also from circulation, interlibrary loan, and other public service departments. Establish close working relationships and understand how your library divvies up e-resources-related work, expertise, and authority among the departments. For example, if your role does not include maintaining 856 fields or MARC records, identify the cataloger who does that work and create channels to communicate issues, request help or information, and track projects.

Leverage Backend System Tools and Capabilities

The more advanced elements of core library systems offer tools to help with implementation and maintenance. For example, integrated library systems (ILSes), LibGuides and LibApps, and most knowledgebases and ERMSes have options for global search and replace or offer the capability to bulk export, edit, and reimport data. Learn backend systems with special attention to tools for managing e-resources efficiently.

Leverage Standards

The National Information Standards Organization (NISO), the ISSN International Centre, the International DOI Foundation, and other organizations have produced many standards and recommended practices that benefit e-resources and core library systems. KBART is a good example of a standard that is useful for e-resources maintenance. KBART codifies the file structure and data elements for sending e-resource titles to knowledgebase providers. Some publishers put KBART files of package contents on pages for library staff, and some have KBART-formatted files with holdings specific to each customer. KBART automation allows the publisher to automatically manage the customer's holdings in its link resolver, turning titles on or off and customizing years held to match the customer's current entitlements.

As e-resources management and the information ecosystem evolve, new problems are identified and new standards are proposed and developed. Stay abreast of existing and forthcoming standards that can boost efficiency, increase usability, and improve e-resources and core library systems.

Use Internal Notes to Document Changes and Activities

If you do something to a e-resource or collection, you will likely do it again or need to *un*do it later. For example, if your main authentication system stops working for a specific database, you may be able to revise the database's URL to use a different authentication method. If your database list allows you to enter an internal note, you can note the change, the date, and the former URL. Once you have resolved the problem, you will have the information needed to restore the original URL. If the system does not allow notes, you can make use of emails, appointments in your calendar, or your choice of a project management tool to note the change and track the resolution.

Notes are useful in many contexts, such as in order records to note the reason for closure, the change of vendor, and so on; in MARC records to note that a title is part of a particular collection, such as a demand-driven acquisitions set; or in the knowledgebase to indicate why a title or package is enabled or disabled for linking. When setting a note, be sure you know whether it is internal only or displays to the public, and whether the note text is searchable. If it isn't searchable and you need to act on it later, consider one of the above additional ways of tracking the information.

Create Workflows and Set Reminders

E-resource maintenance involves many steps and often many people with many tasks repeating annually or more often. Develop workflows and set reminders so that tasks don't get forgotten or abandoned. Modern ILSes and ERMSes support workflows, but with uneven ability to automate task assignments and send reminders. Determine a functional approach in your setting to track the status of e-resources tasks. You can use something as simple as a once-a-month appointment in your calendar to remind you to change the guest password for walk-in access to databases. You can use modern project management and productivity tools, like Trello, Asana, or Airtable, to track rolling out a new EZproxy server. Or, you can set a workflow and a reminder in your ILS to initiate a license review nine months in advance of the expiration of a three-year agreement. Pick the tool that is available and best suited to the specific need, so long as it ensures the tasks stay on track.

Create Documentation for Procedures

Document tasks that are delegated or completed by different people, that involve many steps or decisions, or that need to be completed the same way every time. Documentation can be especially useful if the procedure is complicated enough that you might forget steps or reasons for doing things a particular way. Additionally, documentation can also help you explain procedures to people outside of the e-resources work team who need to understand decisions or outcomes. For example, documenting how the library reports the number of subscribed online journals will help keep the number relatively stable from year to year and prepare you to explain what the number means to administrators. Documenting an online journal package check-in procedure lets you delegate the task to staff as they have free time, and makes it easier to repeat the steps even if it has been a year or two since the last e-journals check-in. Update the documentation as the systems and content change, and share the documentation somewhere accessible to everyone who may need to use or review it.

PROACTIVE MAINTENANCE AND TROUBLESHOOTING

Change is a constant for e-resources collections and core library systems. E-resources management staff need to use proactive maintenance to keep e-resources accurately represented and working for users in core library systems. We actively monitor vendor communications and respond as needed, systematically check links and holdings to improve accuracy, and discover problems and resolve them. Even with proactive maintenance, some problems will arise. Samples and Healy describe proactive troubleshooting as troubleshooting access problems before they are identified by a library user and reactive troubleshooting as investigating and fixing problems after they are discovered and reported by library users and staff (Samples & Healy, 2014). Proactive and reactive responses are a regular part of maintaining access to e-resources. There are many predicable changes and commonplace problems that you will learn to prepare for and respond to.

FINDING OUT ABOUT E-RESOURCES CHANGES AND PROBLEMS

Vendor Communications

Vendors are the main source of information about e-resources. On a regular basis, they send invoices, title lists, and product information and marketing, which may provide details about content additions and title changes. Vendors typically notify customers via email prior to planned changes to content, platforms, access options, or functionality, in advance of the changes, giving libraries time to prepare. However, the library's response often must wait until after the vendor makes changes, which complicates timing. So that the changes are remembered, set up some way to track future tasks and to send yourself reminders, such as in your preferred task or project manager tool, calendar appointments or tasks, or workflows in your ERMS. Another complication in responding to vendor emails is that vendors send the same announcement to every customer. The emails are usually not specific to your subscriptions. For example, you may get a notification with a list of titles that were sold (i.e., transferred) to a different publisher, with no indication of whether your library subscribed to packages that include any of the listed titles.

Subscription Agents

Subscription agents supply information about journal changes of all kinds—format, title, and rate changes, package migrations, and more. Agents send emails and host pages on their admin website where customers can review and download spreadsheets of recent changes. The subscription agent notifications are more likely to be specific to your library's subscriptions.

Library Consortia

Library consortia often share key communications about e-resources, especially relating to subscriptions and vendors managed by the consortia. Consortia may offer different levels of service, from communication tools for discussing problems with other consortium members, to providing a help service to submit problem tickets. In some cases, the consortium may completely take on the troubleshooting, complete any necessary communications with vendors, and make updates to links, records, and knowledgebases.

Discussion Lists

Online discussion lists may alert you to problems and changes that other libraries are dealing with and, quite often, supply ideas and solutions. Two especially helpful lists are ERIL-L (http://www.eril-l .org) and EZproxy-L (https://www.oclc.org/support/services/ezproxy /documentation/list.en.html). ERIL-L discussions explore all aspects of e-resources management work. EZproxy-L focuses on asking for and receiving advice about EZproxy implementations, especially database stanzas. Even if you aren't an EZproxy customer, the list may alert you to functionality that uses a new domain name or otherwise drops authentication. OpenAthens launched a customer discussion list (https://openathens.org/resources/openathens-listserv/) in 2021, which likely will prove important for OpenAthens customers. Monitor these lists as well as ILS- and content-related discussion lists, and platform vendors' sites and discussion lists, to learn about problems and fixes.

Problem Report Forms

Problem reports from library users are a source for learning about temporary glitches, unannounced permanent changes by a vendor, a mismatch between vendor-enabled access and library records, and myriad other issues that interfere with use of core library systems and content. To enable users to easily report issues, incorporate a "Report a Problem" link on key pages, such as on the authentication form, the link resolver menu, the discovery system, and the database list. The "Report a Problem" form can ask the user which content they were trying to access and request their email address if they want to be contacted. Set the form to capture the referring URL, IP address, and browser used, so you have more context and information for troubleshooting.

COUNTER and Usage Data for Spotting Problems

Low usage data can point to problems with access, such as not fully enabling a package in the link resolver or forgetting to turn it on in the discovery layer. Turnaway reports can reveal either gaps in the collection or situations where the vendor has failed to enable access to content your library purchased. Sudden shifts in COUNTER usage may indicate that some part of the library core systems isn't functioning properly or, conversely, that a problem has been resolved. Gather and monitor COUNTER reports at least twice per year, and more often for resources you want to actively track. Chapters 7 and 8 delve further into options for gathering COUNTER reports and their use in renewals.

Web analytics may reveal that traffic isn't coming from expected channels. User testing and focus groups may reveal confusing or broken navigation. Use a variety of methods to check that the e-resources systems are working as you intend. Apply consistent methods of gathering data from year to year and keep notes of incidents that cause a shift in the numbers, such as a transition to a new COUNTER Code of Practice version, implementing a new discovery service or link resolver, and other changes to technology.

CHANGES INITIATED BY PUBLISHERS AND CONTENT PLATFORM VENDORS

Publishers continually expand and refine their content offerings, change titles, transfer titles, and otherwise revise content. Content platform vendors, likewise, continuously update the features of their systems.

Commonplace vendor-initiated changes:

- content additions and removals
- new data sources for the discovery service or knowledgebases
- journal title and ISSN changes
- journal migrations
- database name changes
- platform updates and migrations

Content Additions and Removals

New databases and journals may be added to the collection without the library making a purchase. The processes for implementing new e-resources described in the previous chapter can be used for new online content, whether acquired through a purchase, lease, gift, or other means. You may need to update your ILS, ERMS, link resolver, database list, and authentication service. If the new content is on a new platform, you may need to use the vendor's admin module to add library branding, associated IP ranges, link resolver, and other settings.

If the content is free or acquired through special circumstances, consider adding notes to the ILS to explain the circumstances. Associate the new content with the appropriate license in the ERMS if that information will be needed for renewals. Send announcements to library staff who may be interested.

Removed content requires you to update all the systems where you added the content, removing, suppressing, or editing the records. If the content was associated with a fee, you may need to close purchase records. For journals where the previous issues will still be accessible, leave the links to the title but remember to close holdings statements. If users are likely to continue to look for the removed content, consider leaving a record with the title and a note that the content was removed and why, but remove the links. Send announcements to library staff who may be interested.

New Data Sources

Discovery service vendors regularly add new data sources to the discovery index, and new packages and titles are often added to the link resolver knowledgebase. Check the new sources to determine if they are suitable additions to enable for your users or relevant to your full text collections. If your library subscribes to the added data source, you most likely will want to turn it on for searching in your discovery layer. Verify that the content is a good fit for the discovery interface and that the metadata is of sufficient quality for discovery and linking.

Your decision about whether to enable new sources in your core library systems should take into consideration the metadata quality and relevance to your users' needs. Rich, descriptive metadata with accurate citation data and identifiers support discovery and linking. Thin metadata may not be sufficient for discovery, and records that lack key citation data and identifiers will have problems using connections to full text via the link resolver.

Journal Title and ISSN Changes

As any serials manager will tell you, title changes are a never-ending aggravation. ISSNs, holdings, and URLs may change in conjunction with the title. At minimum, you will need to make sure that the title is changed in the ILS and will need to track the change in the ERMS, update the link resolver knowledgebase, and update links to the title throughout the core library systems if the title's URL changed.

Fortunately, catalogers have well established methods for managing serial title changes in the ILS. Contact your catalogers about the title change or follow normal procedures for closing the old title and starting the new one in the ILS. Tracking the changes in the ERMS and knowledgebase is far less standardized. Add the new title to the ERMS and place notes on the new and old records as needed.

Vendors have an unfortunate habit of consolidating all the prior titles and ISSNs under the newest title and ISSN. They often remove the old titles and ISSNs from the browse and search list. On the vendor's site, check that both the new and prior titles are listed and accessible as your rights allow. Report the problem to the vendor and consider adding the most recent ISSN on the old title and holdings in your ILS. Many link resolver knowledgebases cross-reference prior and current titles and ISSNs. They can often use the current and prior ISSNs to link to the full run of a journal, but not with 100% success. Test the OpenURL links from some citations to the previous and current title. Report linking failures to your link resolver vendor. Also, check links to the journal in core library resources and make any needed updates.

Some publishers use a different domain name for every journal, necessitating a host statement in the EZproxy stanza for each journal on the publisher's platform. When the publisher adds a title, be sure to update the stanza to include the new host statement.

Journal Title Migrations

Journals move between publishers with surprising frequency. Title migrations may happen at any time of the year. Most frequently, you will learn about a transfer during journal renewals. You can proactively monitor the Transfer Alerting Service (https://journaltransfer.issn.org/) provided by NISO and the ISSN International Centre. When titles transfer between publishers, you may need to update the vendor data in acquisitions records; links in your bib records; licensing, URLs and other elements in your ERMS; and packages and holdings in your knowledgebase. Journal package licenses may require you to maintain subscriptions for transferred titles, and you may notice price increases, changes to available formats, and other differences from the previous agreement.

In addition to the work and considerations above, transfers have implications for perpetual rights. Long-term tracking of perpetual rights and licensed holdings is convoluted. Migrated journals might be available partially on the old publisher's platform and partially (or fully) on the new platform. Libraries rely on a combination of ad-hoc tools and information sources to document the licensed titles, entitlements, and perpetual rights:

- the OpenURL knowledgebase
- notes in the ILS or ERMS
- copies of license agreements and title lists
- subscription agent records and systems
- spreadsheets
- email archives

If there's a question about rights, you may need to contact publishers or subscription agents, and consult licenses and paid invoices, to clarify which journals and holdings the library has rights to and on which platform.

Content Platform Migrations and Updates

Database and content vendors continuously improve their interfaces. The small changes usually don't require any response from libraries. Larger changes to the databases' functionality warrant a review to check that everything works and to enable any desired new capabilities. Review the new features to decide which features to implement and how to best implement them.

Major updates and platform migrations require much more attention and work. Publishers may migrate to a new platform or revamp their existing platform every five to seven years. Libraries with multiple e-resource vendors may experience several content platform migrations per year. Platform migrations are particularly at risk of running into some hitches. Publishers may not adequately consider how the new platform will work with authentication, security protocols, link resolvers, embedded search forms, and links in pre-existing library records. Even simple migrations from HTTP to HTTPS can lead to unexpected difficulties (See Appendix C for details of HTTPS problems).

Vendors often send information in advance of a major migration, including a timeline, instructions for updating EZproxy stanzas, and information about the new URLs, and any planned overlap for the old and new platform. Follow any provided instructions to prepare for the migration. Contact your link resolver vendor so that it is aware of the migration. Alert catalogers and others who may need to update links, especially if URLs in the 856 field of a MARC record or permalinks need to change. When the new platform becomes available, test each major feature on campus and off. Be alert to any problems with missing content, dropped proxy, incorrect holdings indicators or access, broken links or branding images, and missing or broken OpenURLs.

Functionality to test on the new platform includes:

- authentication
- searching

- browsing
- results display
- selecting results
- viewing detailed records
- accessing full text
- navigation elements
- OpenURL links
- completeness of entitled content
- library branding

NISO released the Content Platform Migration (CPM) Recommended Practice for comment in spring 2021 (https://www.niso.org/standards-committees/content-platform-migrations). The CPM Recommended Practice introduces key concepts, defines terms, summarizes related standards, and, most importantly, provides recommendations for publishers, platform vendors, library staff, and other stakeholders for each phase of the process. Any library or vendor preparing to migrate content will find the document helpful for organizing and following through on all the steps involved in the project.

ILS and Core Systems Migrations

Library core systems, like other e-resources platforms, also regularly add new functionality, and libraries do change their ILS, ERMS, discovery service, authentication service, and other core systems, though thankfully less frequently than most commercial vendors. Catalogs, discovery service systems, and link resolvers are high-profile, high-use components of the library's online presence. Before any major change, consult public services, subject librarians, web administrators, and systems personnel for guidance and advice. Implementing a new core library system is beyond the scope of this chapter, but the NISO CPM Recommended Practice and some other concepts from this section do apply to some aspects of library core system migrations.

MAINTAINING LINKS

Even if you diligently follow vendor notifications and update links as directed, broken links are likely to creep into your sites. To stave off link rot, you need to respond to vendor-initiated changes, fix reported link problems, and systematically check links throughout library systems.

To respond to vendor-initiated URL changes, you need to:

- Determine which resources are affected. If the vendor migrated to a new platform, all the resources from the vendor will be affected.
- Get new working URLs for the affected resources. The previous chapter describes approaches to finding URLs for resources.
- Test the new URLs on and off site and adjust the authentication services, such as EZproxy stanzas, as needed. See the EZproxy section below for more guidance.
- Search by the old domain name in the library core systems to find all occurrences, including deep links, permalinks, and proxied versions of the old URL.
- Update the links in persistent URL systems, such as the friendly URLs in LibGuides.

PURLs

Persistent URLs (PURLs) allow you to create a URL that remains the same even when the direct URL for a resource changes. To use PURLs, you need to have a service that lets you create the PURL and associate it with the direct URL, and that receives incoming link requests and redirects them to the direct URL. The PURL potentially can be used as the e-resources link in core library systems and throughout the information ecosystem, such as in database lists, in 856 fields in the catalog, in HTML on the website, in LibGuides, in emails and newsletters, and on external sites, such as the learning management system.

PURLs reduce the work involved in maintaining e-resource links. Wherever you link to a resource, use the PURL in place of the direct URL. When you need to update the direct URL, you only have to change it one place—the PURL system. In addition, most PURL systems can incorporate the authentication stem into the PURL, so the resulting link will first prompt the user to log in if they are off campus.

Deep Links, Permalinks, and DOIs

Subject guides and course pages often link to book chapters, articles, videos, and images. These links bypass the intended entry page, connecting to content deeper on the platform. If the deep link was created by copying the URL from the address bar, there is a high likelihood that it includes session IDs that expire, or relies on context or ASPX scripts that aren't represented in the URL. Such URLs are likely to expire and break. Students and faculty may not be aware that the URL will expire, and they may use the address URL as links in the library's pages, resulting in a broken link.

Sample URL including a session ID:

http://a.database.com/record/detail?vid=1&**sid=a952e835-2628 -48ec-97c1-47b40907a3d4%40**&AN=9860303

Fortunately, many database and journal platforms offer permalinks for records, articles, chapters, and even searches. Permalinks are ideal for use in course pages and subject guides. In some cases the permalink will include the proxy authentication stem, and in others it will not, so you may need to add it after creating the link. During link checking, as you discover broken deep links, replace the link with a permalink, if possible. If a permalink isn't feasible, consider using the main e-resources link along with the steps the user should take to get to the deep content. Provide guidance about creating links and offer to help library staff and faculty as needed to reduce the number of broken deep links.

Most modern journal articles and a growing number of books and other formats have a Digital Object Identifier (DOI). Any valid DOI can be used to link to the article or content on the owning vendor's platform. Simply place the valid DOI after the DOI resolver URL.

Sample DOI link: https://doi.org/10.1109/5.771073

The DOI resolver does not incorporate any proxy or authentication, so you must add it as needed. A potential issue with using the DOI is that it will resolve to the publisher that currently owns the content, which can change over time. Your licensed access might be from a different platform than what is linked to by the DOI resolver.

Link Checkers

Link checkers do just what their name implies—they automatically request each URL in the list or on the site and report the links that fail to load a valid page. Link checkers don't assess whether the loaded page is the one you intend—they monitor for HTML error codes. Common error codes include "Page Not Found" (status code 404), "Service Unavailable" (503), and "Timeout" (408 and 504). A more complete list of status codes is available on the Dead Link Checker website (http://www.deadlinkchecker.com; see the "Your Guide to Error Codes"section) and in the Wikipedia entry "List of HTTP Status Codes" (https://en.wikipedia.org/w/index.php?title =List_of_HTTP_status_codes).

Springshare's LibGuides, Drupal, and WordPress have link checkers with added tools for scheduling when links will be checked; specifying which pages, sites, and links will be checked; and for working with the broken link reports to fix links. The exact functions of the link checker vary from service to service. Springshare's link checker has a notable limitation, in that it runs only on links created via the asset entry forms (database assets, link assets, or books from the catalog assets). It does not check links entered in freeform HTML on guides. Use an alternate method, such as a free link checker, to check the rest of the links in the guides and consider replacing the freeform links with link assets.

Several free online link checkers can be found by searching the web. Two examples with impressive functionality are Broken Link Checker (https://www.brokenlinkcheck.com/) and the aforementioned Dead Link Checker. They scan single sites or entire domains, report error codes for all bad URLs, and don't require downloading or installing any software. Free checkers may have for-fee premium features such as automated link checking.

Of course, the next step after finding broken links is to fix or remove the link. The simplest option is to replace a bad link with a working one. Sometimes additional work is needed. For example, the link may break because the database no longer exists in the prior form. You may need to investigate to find out why the link is broken and the best way to fix it. Remember that the same resource is likely to be included in several systems. If the link is broken in one place, it may need to be fixed in several core library system and course pages.

MAINTAINING AUTHENTICATION AND ACCESS SYSTEMS

IP authentication is the most widely used authorization method. Vendors keep records of the IP ranges for each of their customers, and when a request for content comes from a valid IP address, the vendor knows which library the request came from, checks the access entitlements for that customer, and delivers the content. Of course, some vendors prefer username and password access or require customer IDs in addition to IP address. You will need to keep your vendors up to

Figure 6.4
Sample Output From a Broken Link Checker Scan of the University of Central Florida Libraries' Website (https://library.ucf.edu), Completed on February 16, 2018

#	Broken link (you can scroll this field left-right)	Page where found	Server response
1	http://tampabayhistorycenter.org/exhibits/temporary-exhibits/	url src	404
2	https://giving.ucffoundation.org/SSLPage.aspx?pid=558	url src	404
3	http://ucffoundation.planningyourlegacy.org	url src	404
4	http://guides.ucf.edu/2016forum	url src	404
5	http://guides.ucf.edu/c.php?g=78644&p=518083	url src	404
6	https://online.ucf.edu/support/webcourses/turnitin/	url src	404
7	http://guides.ucf.edu/GrantsFundersGuide/NIH_Resources	url src	404
8	http://guides.ucf.edu/GrantsFundersGuide/NSF_Resources	url src	404
9	http://guides.ucf.edu/GrantsFundersGuide/Foundation_Resources	url src	404
10	https://print.ucf.edu	url src	bad host
11	http://ucf.libcal.com/booking/equipment	url src	404
12	http://bot.ucf.edu/minutes/	url src	404
13	http://t.umblr.com/redirect?z=http%3A%2F%2Fwww.cah.ucf.edu%2Fcitizencurator%2F&t=I »	url src	400
14	http://guides.ucf.edu/readingchallenge	url src	404

Status
COMPLETED!
Processed 2031 web pages, found 14 broken links

date with your institution's IP range. If your IP addresses do change, you need to inform every vendor, either using the admin module or sending emails. Use a checklist of contacts to avoid omitting any. The IP Registry acts as a clearinghouse for distributing an institution's URLs to vendors. It's free for libraries and easy to use, and there's no downside to setting up and maintaining an account. However, it's not free to publishers and vendors, and many don't participate, so this will not eliminate the need to contact many vendors. If the IP Registry becomes more widely used, and if it expands its service beyond tracking just IP addresses to tracking basic authentication service use per institution, it could be a big time saver.

Maintaining EZproxy

EZproxy has been the dominant method for authenticating users for off-site access to e-resources for decades. The initial setup requires quite a lot of technical work that will involve system personnel or, if your library opts for the hosted version, OCLC. After it's up and working, EZproxy maintenance becomes simpler and is usually the purview of e-resources management staff. You will maintain the starting-point URLs and stanzas (or targets).

Starting-Point URLs

Any database that you want to be available for off-site use needs a starting-point URL. Starting-point URLs combine the EZproxy domain and the database URL. All starting-point URLs send traffic to your EZproxy server and specify the desired database URL as a bit of data. See the example below that depicts a made-up EZproxy server URL (also called proxy stem) and a made-up database URL.

Sample EZproxy starting-point URL:

https://login.ezproxy.library.org/login?url=https://some .database.com

Once the user is authenticated, the proxy requests the page from the database's server. Because the request is coming from the EZproxy server, which will have an IP associated with your library, the vendor's site recognizes the request as authorized and sends the page back to EZproxy. Before EZproxy sends the page to the browser, it rewrites all the URLs on the page to include the proxy, so link clicks will go through the proxy.

Sample EZproxy URL after authentication:

https://some-database-com.ezproxy.library.org/

Database Stanzas

EZproxy uses database stanzas as instructions on which sites to proxy and how to proxy them. The library must keep the stanzas up to date, adding new ones when new content is acquired, and modifying them when vendors change their platforms. OCLC maintains a database stanzas list that provides authoritative stanzas from many vendors (https://www.oclc.org /support/services/ezproxy/documentation/db.en.html).

Set a schedule to regularly check for new versions of stanzas—vendors often update them without informing libraries. The EZproxy-L discussion list also supplies many stanzas, often incorporating changes to resolve problems that libraries encountered.

The stanzas are incorporated into the targets section of the config.txt file. The simplest stanzas have only two lines: title and URL. Most stanzas also include lines for host and domain.

Hypothetical stanza:

```
T Some Database Title
U https://some.databaseurl.com
HJ alternate.databaseurl.com
DJ databaseurl.com
```

If the publisher has not supplied a stanza, you can construct one based on the title and URL. The online EZproxy documentation provides readable, easy-to-follow guidance on database stanzas. In reality, many of the database stanza are 20 lines long or more and include complicated statements to control use of cookies, to search and replace segments of URLs and other HTML elements, and to perform functions that only the EZproxy gurus understand.

The config.txt file also includes essential settings for EZproxy that are both cryptic and fragile. For the sake of protecting the more technical portions of config.txt, you can put the target stanza statements in their own file or files and use the Include command to pull the files into the setup when EZproxy starts. The included files should be in the same directory as the config.txt file and must be the .txt file type.

Dropped Proxy and Host Errors

Sometimes platforms use scripts or pass through several URLs in response to a browser request. If the script or the sequence includes a URL with a domain name that isn't in the database stanza, the proxy may drop, leaving the user in an unauthenticated view of the vendor's page. When users report that they logged in to the proxy but get paywalls or messages that they aren't a subscriber, check the browser's address bar. If the proxy isn't included, a dropped proxy is a likely cause, and the EZproxy stanza needs to be revised. As mentioned earlier, platform migrations increase the risk of this type of error.

Host errors arise when a starting-point URL includes a database URL that isn't covered by any stanza.

Sample host error:

```
Please contact your library and provide the
name of the resource you were trying to ac-
cess and the Host line below so the library
can correct this error.
Host https://some.url.net
```

Open-access content does not need to be proxied and typically does not have database stanzas, so adding the proxy stem to the OA URLs will result in a host error. Simply remove the proxy stem to fix the problem. Conversely, the database may need to go through the proxy, but no stanza has been entered into the configuration files. You need to find or create a stanza to add.

Maintaining OpenAthens

OpenAthens and Shibboleth are gaining traction for library authentication. Both rely on identity federations and use the Security Assertion Markup Language (SAML) to authenticate and authorize users based on user attributes. The technical work involved with implementing federated identity authentication and establishing new SAML connections is complex and involves institution-wide decisions about user attribute settings, sharing policies, and other decisions usually made outside of the library. In the United States, many higher education and research institutions implemented Shibboleth, but, because of the implementation complexities and other reasons, it was seldom used for library authentication. Because Shibboleth isn't widely used and is quite technical, the details of creating Shibbolized URLs and maintaining connections are not a good fit for this book.

OpenAthens is run by Jisc, as was Athens before it, and was created specifically for library authentication. As such, it is widely used by libraries in the United Kingdom. OpenAthens is now available to libraries in the U.S., with support available via EBSCO and Ovid, and its customer base is expanding rapidly.

OpenAthens redirector URLs are similar to EZproxy URLs. They start with a OpenAthens redirector stem that includes the library's customer ID, followed by the target URL the user wishes to access after authentication. OpenAthens admin includes a link generator to create known working links to vendor resources enabled by the library. The link generator always incorporates URL encoding to replace punctuation with U.S. ASCII codes.

Sample OpenAthens redirector URLs with and without URL encoding:

https://go.openathens.net/redirector/somelibrary.edu?url=https://some.database.com

https://go.openathens.net/redirector/ucf.edu?url=https%3A%2F%2Fsome.database.com

In the past, OpenAthen URLs for some vendors required different URLs structures, such as proxy stem URLs or WAYFless URLs.

Sample OpenAthens proxy stem URL:

https://proxy.openathens.net/login?qurl=https%3A%2F%2Fsome.database.com%2F&entityID=https%3A%2F%2Fidp.library.edu%2Fopenathens

Once authenticated, OpenAthens relies on session cookies to track the user's authentication status. If the target vendor supports SAML-based authentication, then the OpenAthens stem is removed and the URL for the connection is https://some.database.com. However, some vendors don't support SAML. For those connections, OpenAthens acts as a proxy, and the resulting links incorporate the OpenAthens domain.

Sample OpenAthens proxied URL:

https://some-database-com.eu1.proxy.openathens.net/

As you can see from the above sample URLs, core library systems can easily end up with several link styles for OpenAthens authenticated content. The variation will complicate maintaining the URLs or setting a global authentication method in core library systems. Pick a preferred link style, usually the redirector link with or without URL encoding, and use it as consistently as possible. When you encounter alternate-style OpenAthens links, check to see if the URL can be updated to your preferred style.

OpenAthens Admin

The OpenAthens admin system has many components that may be maintained by the e-resources management staff, the IT department, or a combination of the two. Turning on OpenAthens access for a given vendor takes two steps. The vendor has your OpenAthens identity information. This step is analogous to telling the vendor your IP range—it lets them know how to recognize your users.

Typical OpenAthens identity information:

Identity: Library or University Name
EntityID: https://idp.library.edu/openathens
Federation Scope: https://idp.library.edu/openathens
OpenAthens Org ID: 12345678

The next step is to enable the vendor in the OpenAthens resources catalog. Enabling the vendor in the Resources Catalog is analogous to adding a database stanza into the EZproxy configs, in effect, but far simpler to accomplish, in practice. If a needed resource isn't listed in the resources catalog, contact your OpenAthens support service to request the additions. Additions may take a day or more to complete. Applying the OpenAthens redirector to a resource that isn't enabled in the Resource Catalog will result in a "Forbidden" error page.

OpenAthens admin has controls for setting up user accounts, mapping user attributes to permission sets, associating resources with permission, customizing a My OpenAthens page for your library, and reviewing usage data. If you are the administrator for one or more of these aspects of OpenAthens, become familiar with the options. If you create user accounts, note their expiration dates and set up reminders to perform any actions needed on a recurring basis.

Authenticating New E-Resources

When you add new e-resources, you may need to create starting-point URLs wherever you decided to add a direct link to the database. Consider using a PURL or FriendlyURL instead of using direct links. Link resolvers, some PURL systems, and some ILSes allow you to enter the authentication stem into the system once, then apply it to any database by checking a box. This method has many advantages, including reducing problems from typos, and it enables easy updates to the proxy stem globally when your library changes the authentication service or proxy server domain name.

MAINTAINING ONLINE JOURNALS

The library's accessible journal content results from a combination of licenses and subscription models. The rights to the journals vary, from perpetual access rights to no guarantee of access at all. The list below includes common sources of access to journal content.

Journal acquisition sources include:

- library-subscribed individual journals
- subscription journals in packages
- access-only titles or years in a package
- purchased archives and perpetual rights titles
- open-access journals (gold, hybrid, bronze, green, diamond)
- consortium-subscribed journals
- journal full-text content in aggregator databases

(See Chapter 3 for more information about acquisition scenarios.)

Smooth access to full-text journal articles requires accurate titles and holdings, and working links. You need to track packages, titles per package, holdings per title, and licensed access type. Some titles may be available from more than one package, with different holdings and different license terms from each package. Complications also arise from journal title changes, ISSN changes, and the potential for titles to disappear from aggregator, open-access, and free-access sources.

Inevitably, titles and holdings on library sites can become uncoordinated with the titles on the initial license, renewal invoices, and vendor sites. The mismatch can result in bad links that lead to error pages and paywalls. The opposite can occur, as well, with vendors providing content that the library fails to link to from its sites. Systematic maintenance can realign all the titles and holdings across the core library systems and vendor sites.

E-Journal Check-in

An e-journal check-in process is modeled after physical journal check-in, where each journal's holdings are updated and the library verifies it has the content. For e-journals, the process compares the titles on an invoice with the ILS, knowledgebase holdings and journal list, and content accessible on the vendor platform.

Appendix A provides a sample e-journal check-in process. You can adjust it to fit the needs of your library. The process is time consuming and meticulous. Most libraries will not find it feasible to check in the entire collection every year. The process may be made more manageable by cycling through the collection, checking one or two packages every year, or focusing on packages that changed or titles identified as having problems.

Another way to check journal title lists and holdings is to compare data from two or more sources that all include ISSNs or other matching data points. Potential data sources include invoices, exports from the ILS, vendor KBART files, COUNTER reports, link resolver, or ERMS. Load each dataset into separate Microsoft Excel worksheets and use MATCH or VLOOKUP formulas to match ISSNs from each dataset. You may need to clean and normalize the ISSNs, and be mindful of whether the match is checking print ISSNs, eISSNs, or both. Rarely does the process cleanly match all the titles, but it can provide a good start for identifying titles missing from one or more data sources and for consolidating data from different sources.

Aggregators are the source for thousands of journals, with varying holdings. If you load MARC records for aggregator full text, you need a plan to update the records set very frequently. Some libraries purchase MARC records from their link resolver vendor, and MARC records are updated along with the resolver's knowledgebase.

Complications from Access-only and Open Access

Access-only and open access are a boon for researchers but cause confusion when trying to align access with licensed titles. Libraries often enable the content in their link resolver, online journals list, and catalog. However, the content is more prone to becoming inaccessible or changing without notice, for reasons explained below. From the user's perspective, it appears that the library suddenly dropped access to content. Library staff need to investigate the cause of the lost access. Frequently, the reason isn't easily apparent from looking at any one source, such as the vendor site or subscription agent information.

Open access (OA) content constitutes an important component of almost every library's journal collection. Current estimates show 28% of scholarly articles have some form of OA version available (Piwowar et al., 2018). Gold and bronze open access are especially relevant for journals checking and troubleshooting.

> Gold OA: Gold OA journals are completely free to access, and the articles usually have a Creative Commons license that commits the publisher to keeping the content open (though not to host the content) in perpetuity. Many gold OA journals are published by commercial vendors and are frequently funded through article processing charges (APCs).

> Bronze OA: Piwowar et al. use the term "bronze OA" to refer to articles that are "free to read on the publisher page, but without a clearly identifiable license." The publishers are not obligated to continue providing the free access. Bronze OA is very common, and even more prevalent than gold open access (2018).

Gold OA journals may cease or make changes that break links without any prior notice. They may or may not have a host for the content if the publisher abandons the journals. Bronze OA presents the challenge of the library having to stumble upon or systematically check for free content, and also having to check if the free access is converted to subscription only or if the content is removed. Bronze OA may look indistinguishable from access-only on subscription vendor sites. For both types of OA, the publisher is unlikely to send notices about any changes. The systematic e-journals check-in procedure in Appendix A works for uncovering changes to gold and bronze OA sources.

"Access-only" usually means journals and holdings that your library has licensed access to through a journal package deal, but that are not your core subscriptions within the package. Often, but not always, libraries pay a per-title subscription fee for core journals in a package and have perpetual rights to the core titles for the years during which the library paid a subscription. The access-only titles typically have no per-title fee and no perpetual rights. Once the deal ends, or if the title migrates to a different publisher, the access-only titles or holdings become inaccessible.

For example, consider a situation where a library subscribes to Package X that includes *Journal A* and *Journal B*. The library subscribes to Package X from 2006 to 2016. From 2006 to 2016, the library pays a subscription fee for *Journal A*, and gets *Journal B* for no fee as access-only. The package deal provides access to the journals from 1999 to current for both titles. If the library cancels the deal in 2017, the library continues to have access to 2006 to 2016 issues of *Journal A*, but loses all access to *Journal B* and to the 1999 to 2005 content for *Journal A*.

Perpetual Rights and Archives

Journal licenses frequently provide post-termination access to the content, called perpetual rights, which allow continued access to the titles for the years your library paid for subscriptions. Tracking perpetual rights entitlements is challenging. The title list may change yearly, and ERMSes and other tools don't have a mechanism for tracking which titles in a package come with perpetual rights versus which titles are accessible only for the subscription period. Each library may have its own approach, using notes in the ILS or ERMS, spreadsheets, invoices, and licenses. When a library opts to drop a subscription, it may have continued access to the perpetual rights on the vendor's site, or it may have to find some other method of hosting the content securely. Records and holdings for the canceled title need to be updated, as described earlier in this chapter, and the source for continued access to the perpetual rights content needs to be found and turned on.

LOCKSS and CLOCKSS support post-cancellation access to some titles for participating libraries. Portico also supports perpetual access, with a slightly different model. Portico started as a "dark archive," meaning that it harvests full text and stores it but does not make the content accessible until a trigger event occurs. The normal trigger is if the publisher or copyright owner ceases to provide any access. Portico then turns on access to the affected titles for the entire world. Portico now offers "grey archive" services as well, supplying post-cancellation access to specific titles for libraries that ceased subscribing but have perpetual rights.

When your library ceases a journal package subscription, check for perpetual rights to some or all of the journals in the package and verify that the vendor is extending the access that is due.

MAINTAINING E-BOOKS

Like the e-journals collection, the e-book collection is an amalgamation of titles purchased from different vendors with different terms. E-book collections may continue to accumulate throughout the year, similar to print book acquisitions. They have the added complication of relatively new acquisition models and unusual access models.

Libraries acquire e-books by purchasing them:

- from publishers, individually or as a package
- from aggregators, individually or as a package
- as package subscriptions from aggregators
- as package subscriptions from publishers
- via demand-driven acquisition (DDA), also called patron-driven acquisition (PDA) and evidence-based acquisition (EBA)
- through consortium-purchased or -subscribed e-books

Additionally, libraries can add and manage open-access e-books.

Libraries acquire e-books as bundled collections and as individual titles (e.g., firm orders), both from the publisher and from e-book aggregators. E-books hosted on the publisher's platform typically have favorable access terms and technologies, such as unlimited simultaneous users (SUs), complete book or chapter downloads, and allowances for printing and copying. They often come with perpetual rights.

E-book aggregator platforms offer books from a variety of publishers, with a variety of access and purchase options. Aggregator-provided e-books usually have options for simultaneous user limits, typically one SU, three SUs, and unlimited SUs, though some vendors replace the unlimited tier with an option of up to some threshold of uses per annum (often 325), with any use beyond that threshold triggering a purchase of an additional copy. Libraries are likely to have e-books from each tier of SU in the collection. Collections purchased by consortia may come with an additional twist, in that the SU allowance may be shared by all participating libraries. A book with 3 SUs might have all three copies in use, each at a different library.

Using books from aggregator platforms is far from straightforward. Aggregator platforms may require users to authenticate to view the content, even from on campus, and may require them to log in with an Adobe Digital Editions account to download the e-book. Some also require an e-book reader app, like Bluefire Reader or Overdrive, for use on a mobile device. The e-book download uses up an SU slot for the loan period, and the content "returns" to the collection automatically when the period is up. Different e-books can have different loan periods.

From the user's perspective, e-book access is confusing and unpredictable. Ideally, the ILS and other locations for discovering the e-books would show the number of allowed simultaneous users, the loan period, and required software and accounts. Notes in the MARC records or loaded to the ILS from the ERMS can help, but first, library staff must create the notes, and then maintain them if the library adds additional SUs. The needed data can be gleaned from the e-book aggregator's admin module and from the book agent's record of purchases. Surprisingly, the information isn't typically displayed in the aggregator platform.

Demand-Driven and Evidence-Based Acquisitions

Demand-driven acquisition (DDA) and evidence-based acquisition (EBA) present additional maintenance challenges for libraries. The typical DDA deal lets library users access a large collection of e-books. Each title can be used, either at no charge or at a fraction of the book's cost, up to some preset threshold, such as number of times used, or percentage of the book's content accessed. Use beyond the threshold triggers an automatic purchase of the book.

Evidence-based acquisition is similar, in that the library gains access to a collection of titles it has not yet purchased, and usage influences purchase decisions. Typically, the library and vendor agree on a period during which the entire set of books will be available and on a total amount the library will spend during or at the end of the period. At the end of the agreed-upon period, the library reviews the usage—the "evidence"—and selects titles to purchase. The library might opt to acquire the most heavily used titles; titles that align with curriculum or program needs, or the needs of researchers or local populations; or any combination of criteria.

As with any e-resource, the library must manage the e-book collections and records in core library systems, making them discoverable and accessible through MARC loads, enabling collections in the ERMS and in discovery systems, and setting up linking. DDA and EBA collections tend to be dynamic—the exact set of titles available is likely to constantly shift during the contract period. At the end of the contract period, the library may decide to remove some or all the records for titles that weren't selected for purchase. Libraries need to plan for the easy identification and removal of the DDA and EBA records; for example, by creating unique database collection identifiers to put in a specific 9XX field in the MARC records for e-books.

While the DDA or EBA is in effect, the library and vendor closely track the use of titles to monitor and control spending and account balances. For purchased titles, the library may choose to replace the brief MARC provided by the vendor with more complete records.

MAINTAINING STREAMING MEDIA

Like e-books, streaming media (e.g., video, audio) are offered in a variety of purchase, subscription, and lease models.

Acquisition sources for streaming media include:

- purchase or lease from publishers, individually or as a package
- purchase or lease from aggregators, individually or as a package
- DDA for purchase or lease
- consortium or affiliate purchase or lease

Online media pose many of the same linking challenges as e-books, with a unique URL for each stream and few good options to use DOIs or the link resolver. They also introduce complications unique to streaming media.

Most streaming media platforms have functionality specific to videos, such as the ability to create clips and playlists, showing closed captions or synchronous transcripts synchronized to the playback, and providing embed codes. The embed codes are a means to insert streaming media in course pages, LibGuides, or any other web page. The codes usually use the <iframe> HTML tag, as shown in the made-up example below. The <iframe> tag may not work in every setting, can be difficult to troubleshoot, and may be impossible to resolve. Look for an option to link to the media, if the embed code does not work.

Sample streaming video embed code:

```
<iframe src="https://ezproxy.university.edu
/login?url=https://search.videovendor.com
/embed/token/04b32oj5eprnoc9n70o34dho"
frameborder="0" width="470" height="390"
allowfullscreen></iframe>
```

Media streaming requires a good internet connection, an up-to-date browser, and, for some platforms, specific video playback support. The services typically work with most modern devices and browsers.

Streaming media have a further complication relating to public performance rights (PPR). Streaming media typically require a license for acquisition, which usually dictates conditions for screening the media to a group, even to stream it to a classroom. Public performance may be explicitly prohibited, allowed, or allowed in specific settings. When you acquire a video or other media, check the license for terms relating to PPR and note them in your ERMS, MARC records, or your records for the package.

Online music and images are typically purchased or subscribed to as collections, rather than single pieces, and are often treated as databases. MARC records may be available for sound recordings and images. Both music and art platforms have custom interfaces customized for their content, with special players or viewers, options to create playlists or slide decks, and capability to embed players in external pages.

MAINTAINING THE DATABASE LIST

Database vendors continue to develop new offerings, re-bundle and re-name content, and migrate to new platforms. Ideally, database vendors will send announcements about any title and link changes. However, sometimes the announcement either goes unnoticed, never reaches e-resources staff, or is never made. In addition to your paid subscription databases, the database list may include titles you have access to through other arrangements.

A library's database list might incorporate:

- library-subscribed databases
- consortium-subscribed databases
- complimentary databases from vendors
- free databases (e.g., AgeLine, ERIC, Medline)
- journal platform top-level links

Consortial or regional deals and agreements with affiliate libraries may provide quite a few databases. Communications from the vendor about changes to the content will likely go to the consortium or library that directly subscribes. You may not receive information about purchase decisions, title and holding changes, or other notifications. You will need to proactively check for changes to the available e-resources provided through these deals.

The list might also include alternate or old titles with referrals to the new titles, links to free web pages, and content that isn't strictly a database. Periodically review the database list contents and revisit decisions about included non-database content.

Occasionally, conduct a database list check that compares the databases on your list with the vendor's pages. Also, periodically skim consortium and affiliated libraries' database pages to see if databases have been added or removed from their lists. Consider adding a note to your list to indicate the consortium or library that provides the sources, to avoid confusion if the resource suddenly disappears or if you are trying to figure out why you have access. A sample database list check procedure is in Appendix B.

Database Name Changes

When a database's name changes, you need to update the database list and core library systems (e.g., the ERMS and ILS). Because users might continue to look for the database under the old title, you may decide to leave the old title in the list with a referral to the new title, or use an "alternate title" field, such as that which is available in Springshare's database list service. If you don't have an alternate title option, rather than creating a new entry for the new title, rename the existing entry and add a new entry for the old title, but with no link to the vendor's site. Instead of a link, add a referral to the new title. It sounds more complicated, but it will reduce the work of updating links, particularly if you use PURLs or FriendlyURLs. The existing PURL will be associated with the new title. Search for occurrences of the old title throughout the library's sites and update the link text to the new title. If the occurrences already use the existing PURL, you don't need to update the link. If the database has a new URL along with the new name, update the direct links and the PURLs accordingly. Test that that the new URL works with EZproxy and update the stanzas if needed.

Alternate Database Lists

Downtime for one or more of the library core technologies doesn't need to mean that e-resources are unavailable to users. Most databases are hosted off site, so even when the database list is down, the actual databases are still available. You can create a failsafe database list that bypasses the library's usual list and provides direct links that bypass the PURL and authentication systems. Host the failsafe on an external server, such as Google Drive, Dropbox, or Box. The failsafe can be as simple as a copy of the database list with direct URLs, or it can include additional information and elements. LibGuides and ERMSes support exporting and can include several elements in an exported list, such as PURLs, proxied URLs, and subjects. You will need to update it monthly or more and make sure library staff know how to get to the alternative list. When the database list site is down, having a browser bookmark and an unobtrusive link on the library site will help library staff quickly guide users to the working list.

MAINTAINING E-RESOURCES SETTINGS IN ADMIN MODULES

While much of the work of keeping access up and working happens in library core systems, you must also control settings and maintain links on the myriad vendor platforms. Larger vendors usually have library admin pages where you can share your IP range, EZproxy stem or OpenAthens data, link resolver base URL and button image, library logo, library name, and so on. Some sites, particularly the large aggregators, allow libraries to customize the search interface, options for user accounts, and more. Admin modules typically provide usage statistics, as well as options to download COUNTER and, perhaps, non-COUNTER reports.

Whatever setting you configure, you must plan to maintain. While IP ranges, authentication services, and link resolver changes don't happen often, when they do, they involve updating settings for a large portion of the core library systems and communicating with nearly all licensed content vendors. Carefully track which systems and vendors need to be updated and the status of each. Visit each admin module to check the settings and stored information. The IP Registry can help libraries communicate their current, accurate IP range information to a small number of participating vendors, but many platforms don't use the IP Registry.

You will need the URL, username, and password for each admin module, and a plan to store and manage them. ERMSes and spreadsheets allow you to share and organize login credentials. Online password managers offer an alternative, with the advantage that they supply the URL and login credentials when and where you need them, in your browser when you want to go to an admin module. LastPass, Bitwarden, and Dashlane are examples of password managers. They provide browser plugins that monitor your interactions with login forms and can create secure passwords, store the URL and credentials when you log in, and, if you change a password on a site, update that information. LastPass can export all the site URLs and credentials as a spreadsheet, so you can have a backup of the information available to all e-resources management staff. LastPass and other password managers have many other features as well. They are well worth considering as an option for organizing and sharing admin module URLs and credentials, especially given that admin module URLs change with surprising frequency.

SKILLS

Understanding the Core Library Systems and Admin Modules

Understand the roles and capabilities of core library systems and their admin modules and backends. Know how the systems interact and connect to each other, especially related to how users transition from one system to another as they conduct research and seek content.

URL Basics

URLs are so fundamental to the functionality of core library systems and e-resources, it's hard to stress enough the need to have a solid grasp of their structure and elements. Develop enough familiarity to understand, troubleshoot, and modify URLs. Whether the URL is as simple as a protocol and domain name, or as complicated as a link resolver (e.g., combining elements to construct a deep link that includes article metadata, a customer ID, and authentication statements), you need to develop the ability to spot problems and the skill to find or create work-ing links.

These two sites deliver very good introductions to URLs and stanzas:

- "Understanding URLs," Goodwill Community Foundation (https://edu.gcfglobal.org/en/internet-tips/understanding-urls/1/)
- "Understanding URLs and database stanzas," OCLC (https://help.oclc.org/Library_Management/EZproxy/EZproxy_configuration/Understanding_URLs_and_database_stanzas?sl=en)

Authentication Basics

Become familiar with the service your library uses for authentication. In most libraries, EZproxy is essential for providing off-site access to e-resources. Even though you may not be involved in all aspects of its con-figuration, become familiar with the functions of the basic files, especially config.txt and user.txt. Learn how to find, construct, and modify database stanzas, and how to respond to host errors and dropped proxy errors. Fol-low discussions on EZproxy-L.

If your library uses OpenAthens, familiarize yourself with OpenAthens admin functionality and keep your library's identity information handy.

COUNTER

Know how to download or acquire COUNTER reports from vendor ad-min modules. Understand the content and purpose of the standard reports, and become familiar with COUNTER 5 terminology and metric types (https://www.projectcounter.org/friendly-guides-release-5/).

Spreadsheets and Data Manipulation

Spreadsheets are widely used by e-resources staff and vendors for orga-nizing, delivering, and storing crucial information. Vendor admin modules, link resolver knowledgebases, ERMSes, and other systems typically support downloading data, such as KBART files, holdings entitlements, invoices, subscription analyses, and COUNTER reports, in spreadsheet-compatible formats. Getting the most out of the various reports requires you to compile data from multiple sources. Often the data is messy and will not work well with Excel MATCH and VLOOKUP functions until you clean and normalize the data, particularly ISSNs, which may be entered as text or as numbers and with or without the hyphen, and may use the print or electronic ISSN as the primary number. Learn to use Excel, OpenRefine, or other data manipulation and cleanup tools well enough that you can clean data. Develop moderately advanced Excel skills so you can produce a variety of reports and calculations based on e-resources data from multiple sources.

CONCLUSION

Maintaining access to e-resources and evaluating the success of that effort comprises most of an e-resources manager's work. The content, platforms, and underlying technologies are in continuous flux. You must keep abreast of the ever-shifting collection and holdings and ensure that your library's representation of accessible content is accurate and complete. You will need to cooperatively maintain the technologies that enable access and create the connections between core library systems and the broader information ecosystem. Monitoring usage and conducting assessments will help you identify successes and problems.

CITATIONS AND FURTHER READING

Samples, J., & Healy, C. (2014). Making it look easy: Maintaining the magic of access. *Serials Review, 40* (2), 105–117. https://doi.org/10.1080/00987913.2014.929483

Samples and Healy discuss the complexity of e-resources management and proactive versus reactive troubleshooting. Proactive troubleshooting refers to finding and re-solving problems before end users encounter and report them and uses techniques such as systematically checking links to e-resources and verifying that holdings are accessible. The authors concluded that most libraries primarily rely on reactive trou-bleshooting, responding to problems reported by users. Both proactive and reactive approaches require broad knowledge of the myriad systems involved in providing access to e-resources, which aren't well understood by staff from other departments in the library.

The article provides an excellent, realistic overview of the state of e-resources main-tenance. The included survey responses give insight into workflows, staffing, and procedures that academic libraries use in responding to e-resources problems.

Hoeppner, A. (2017). Database lists A to Z: A practitioner's tips and caveats for managing database lists. *The Serials Librarian, 73*(1), 27–43. https://doi.org/10.1080/0361526X .2017.1320779

Hoeppner begins by providing an overview of the evolution of database lists from the late 1990s to 2017, showing the growth in the number and types of resources and the improvements in functionality. The majority of the article is a series of prac-tical tips, from deciding what to include to handling title changes and cancellations, and systematically comparing the list with vendor pages.

The article is a good introduction to the issues of and approaches to creating and maintaining a functional database list. One downside is that its description of LibGuides and some related advice was already out of date at the time of publication, as Springshare made significant improvements to its database assets functionality in fall 2017.

With apologies for self-citing.

Norris, T. B., & Suomela, T. (2017). Information in the ecosystem: Against the "informa-tion ecosystem." *First Monday, 22*(9). https://firstmonday.org/ojs/index.php/fm /article/view/6847/6530

Piwowar, H., Priem, J., Lariviere, V., Haustein, A. F., West, J. Matthias, L.; Norlander, B., & Alperin, J. P. (2018). The state of OA: A large-scale analysis of the prevalence and impact of open access articles. *PeerJ, 6*, Article e4375. https://doi.org/10.7717/peerj .4375

Wilson, K. (2017). The knowledgebase at the center of the universe. *The Serials Librarian, 72*(1-4), 111–117. https://doi.org/10.1080/0361526X.2017.1320869

Knowledgebases first gained prominence in libraries as the core of link resolver services. They are essential to e-resources management and discovery. Accord-ing to Wilson, knowledgebases rival the catalog in importance. This article is an excellent overview of knowledgebases, providing a summary of their evolu-tion, creation, content, uses, and innovations. Wilson describes the integration of the knowledgebase with the library service platform, using EBSCO and OCLC as examples.

APPENDIX A: SAMPLE E-JOURNAL CHECK-IN

1. Start with an invoice and use a version of the steps below so you make sure you have turned on the subscriptions that you paid for. This process starts with title and entitlements data from invoices or the subscription agent and checks access and holdings in each system below with corrections made as needed:

   - vendor site
   - LMS/ ILS
   - ERMS
   - link resolver

2. Create a working list of titles to check.
3. Find title and holdings information from one or more source:

   - invoices
   - subscription agents
   - licenses
   - purchased archive title lists

   Merge data from various sources into one spreadsheet for convenience. Useful starting information:

   - title
   - ISSN
   - holding entitlements
   - ILS system number
   - fund code
   - the library's e-journals list

4. Use the public view of the e-journals list to verify that:

- Title is listed.
- Holdings match entitlements/accessible content.
- Link opens to vendor platform.

If not, make corrections in list admin (e.g., the link resolver or ERMS).

Enable the vendor platform, title, and correct holdings as needed. Each system is different enough that it isn't feasible to summarize the process here.

5. Access the content on the vendor's platform. Alternatively, search or browse to find the title on the vendor's site and verify that:

- Title is listed.
- Holdings match entitlements. If holdings exceed entitlements, note the additional free access and consider adding the holdings information to library records.

Open sample full text from most recent and oldest holdings.

If content is missing or hits a paywall:

- Double-check entitlement status.
- Contact publisher and and/or subscription agent.

6. Check the ILS to verify that:

- Title has a bib record in ILS.
- 856 link uses preferred linking method and opens to vendor page.
- Holdings statement matches entitlements/accessible content (if used).
- Title has order/payment record, and payment information matches the invoice.
- ILS and fund code match the invoice.

If any of the above is incorrect or missing, then:

- Ask a cataloger to provide a record.
- Create a new 856 link. Preferably, use an OpenURL, PURL, or similar durable link that also handles proxy or another authentication as needed.
- Edit the holdings to match the accessible/subscribed/purchased/ holdings. Create a payment record and/or investigate to find the previous payment to update or close it. Send the correct ILS and fund code to the vendor or agent.

This sample process can be rearranged and repurposed. Using invoices as a starting point will help you catch titles newly added to a package. However, renewal invoices likely only show the current subscription titles, not previously purchased archive collections or gold or bronze OA titles. To check for these titles, start with the titles list from the vendor's platform, then perform steps 2 and 4 to update the ILS, journals list, and link resolver.

APPENDIX B: DATABASE LIST CHECK PROCEDURE

- Go to or acquire a working list of databases to check.
- Go to each database vendor's platform to see the list of databases. This approach is especially useful for platforms that can host many databases, such as EBSCOhost, Cengage (Gale), and ProQuest.
  Note: Invoices for databases often don't list each database from the vendor. The invoice does indicate that one or more database or e-resource was purchased and should be accessible.
- Use database lists hosted by consortia or other sites where you have rights to all the databases.
- Check that each database on your working list is on the database list.
- Check that the link connects to the right page.
- Check that the link uses the PURL or FriendlyURL.
- If the database is missing, decide if it should be added. Some databases may not be desirable.

- Add the database as you would a newly subscribed database.
- Test the link to the database from on and off site.
- If the link does not work, check the direct URL.
- If it works, check that the proxy is correctly applied.
- If the direct link does not work, find a functional link, as described in the Links section of this chapter, or find out if the database platform is having a problem.
- If the on-site access works but off-site does not, check and update EZproxy stanzas as needed.
- Check that the description, subjects, dates, vendor, and other metadata are correct.
- Fix information about the database as needed. If there are big differences, investigate if content was added or dropped, or if there were other changes.
- Check the ERMS and ILS for the database. Optional.
- Add it if needed or investigate differences.
- Check that the database is enabled in the discovery service index. Optional.

APPENDIX C: HTTP TO HTTPS MIGRATIONS

One common type of platform update is the transition from HTTP to HTTPS (hypertext transfer protocol secure). HTTPS provides increased privacy and data integrity for transactions over the internet. For libraries that use EZproxy, the change usually requires some modification to the proxy stanzas and requires that the proxy have a wildcard SSL certificate. The transition, if done well by the vendor, can be problem-free. The EZproxy-L discussion list provides many examples of problems that arose from publishers switching to HTTPS. Similar to issues that arise from platform migrations, the vendors may miss some details about how HTTPS will affect proxying, links and forms embedded in library pages, and specific functionality.

Figure 6.5
Example of page experiencing HTTPS conflict from the University of Central Florida Libraries' Website

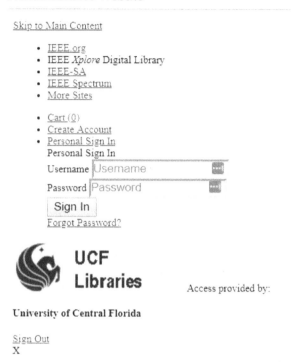

Problems also arise when sites load both secure and unsecure content in the same page. The image in Figure 6.5 is a typical example of a page experiencing some HTTPS conflict. The text of the page loaded, but style elements, most images, and some functionality did not. HTTPS and SSL issues can be quirky and difficult to pin down. Experts on EZproxy-L, your website manager, or your institution's IT staff may be able to help troubleshoot HTTPS conflicts and issues.

APPENDIX D: VENDOR-BLOCKED IPS

Vendors monitor their platforms for unusual activity, such as systemic downloading of journal runs, extremely rapid page access, and just excessively long sessions. When they detect suspicious activity, they respond by blocking the IP address from which the activity originated and notifying the library. The notification includes the IP addresses that were blocked, a description of the activity, a log file, a statement about what action is needed to have the IP restored, and vendor contact information. Investigating the activity requires access to the vendor and local logs, details about the institution's networking and IP address assignments, and user identity management. Most likely, the investigation will involve the institution's network administrators or information security team.

After the investigators identify the computer and user, the library can contact the user. The user may reveal that they weren't directly involved in the incident or that they truly did not know that systematic downloading was prohibited. In many cases, the user's login credentials were compromised and exploited by pirate sites to harvest articles. Some vendors monitor pirate sites that post compromised login credentials and block access to the library's proxy until the compromised accounts are secured.

Sample email from vendor:

"This email is to notify you that we have detected unusual activity on our site, www.journalvendor.com, originating from the following IP address:

123.45.67.89

As a preventive measure, we have blocked this IP address from accessing the site anymore. Please note that this may prevent valid users of your institution from accessing the site if they are coming in from the same IP. To unblock this IP address you must contact the publisher, who will be able to analyze the problem and unblock it.

ATTACHMENT: audit_log.txt"

Steps to respond to blocked IP addresses:

1. Respond to the vendor and initiate investigation.
2. Send the activity log to IT security/networking.
3. When user is identified:
   - Block the user's account from proxy or library logins.
   - Contact the individual and explain that their activity was prohibited.
   - Remove the login block when the user replies, changes their password, and commits to comply with copyright and license terms.
   - Contact the vendor to summarize the findings and library response. Do not divulge the user's information.

Seven

Getting Started with Resource Review

Lindsay Cronk and Anna Creech

Review is a strategic part of the e-resources management process of ongoing evaluation and access, as defined in *TERMS 1.0* and *2.0*, and an annual review offers significant collection assessment and engagement opportunities. As library materials budgets face increasing constraints, a robust review process—conducted at appropriate intervals based on institutionally appropriate criteria—is your best friend. We both recently undertook review of our entire collections due to additional scrutiny during the COVID-19 pandemic, and this chapter draws from experiences in both regular and urgent review. While we focus on an annual review cycle, you can apply the techniques and processes described here at any appropriate interval and/or adapt them to any library setting.

With a tailored resource review process, we assure the rigor and agility of our collections and collection processes. Additionally, we demonstrate to our institutional administrations that the library takes fiscal responsibility seriously, particularly in times when collection budgets are tight. Often, our budgets come into question due to the annual need for increases to keep pace with increasing costs. Being good stewards of our budgets and collections is crucial work on behalf of our users, part of representing and advocating for their interests. It allows us to maximize the limited resources we have to support research and curricular needs.

Implementing a review process may seem daunting, but by starting with a basic framework and then tailoring the system to your library's needs, it can be incrementally improved without overwhelming the library staff involved. It's not necessary to take on every resource immediately, but developing a scalable system will prove invaluable, particularly in times of additional scrutiny. As *TERMS 1.0* notes, "Although it is essential to review all resources, it is often fairly straightforward to renew many resources at a glance" (Emery & Stone, 2013). Our review guidance is intended to provide you with a basis for that work that helps you with both simple and more complicated decision-making.

Critical to the success of any review process is ensuring that there is a person acting in coordination of the process—this chapter assumes that you are that person. The library worker undertaking this work is typically the e-resources librarian or an e-resources staff member, but it could be anyone from collections or acquisitions. Whatever your job title, you're taking up an important process, and we hope to support you in successfully implementing it.

To implement a basic functional review system in your library, you will want to begin by collecting and organizing the following data:

- **e-resource titles, renewal costs, and renewal dates** (resources should be reviewed a minimum of 120 days in advance of the renewal invoice date, to assure that all cancellation or renewal decisions are communicated to vendors ahead of the standard 90-day cancellation clause notification window)
- **e-resource usage statistics** (from the vendor)
- **e-resource qualitative usage data** (from selectors/stakeholders; may be narrative)

DEVELOPING A MODEL FOR REVIEW

To assure an orderly execution of the decision for each e-resource reviewed, you will want to track and notify both the associated library stakeholders (i.e., subject experts or other invested staff members) for decision-making and then notify the e-resource vendor contact. Different intervals for meetings than what is indicated below may be better suited for your stakeholders. In the figures below, two models for an integrated e-resources review system are explored.

Figure 7.1
Model of a Monthly E-Resources Review System

Monthly E-Resources Review

In Figure 7.1, we've visualized a staggered monthly review. In this model, there is a review process each month, which focuses on all renewals four months prior to their renewal date. This model would require monthly processes and communications and makes sure that the resource review process is ongoing and rolling, which can increase the agility of collection processes and the responsiveness of the e-resources portfolio.

Figure 7.2.
Model of a Triannual-Based E-Resources Review System

Triannual Review System

Renewal Month	Review Semester			Review Semester
	Fall	Spring	Summer	Fall
January	●			Spring
February	●			Summer
March	●			
April	●			
May		●		
June		●		
July		●		
August		●		
September			●	
October			●	
November			●	
December			●	

In Figure 7.2, we show a visualization for a staggered semester review. In this model, the review process would occur at semester intervals, and resource review would happen more than six months in advance of the renewal date in some cases. This model requires three intensive data gathering and presentation cycles but allows for renewal decisions to be prepared far in advance of vendor licensing requirements.

Selecting a review interval that serves local needs is key to successfully implementing a review system. A small library with limited staff may find that a criteria-based review process is the best application of its time and resources. Assessing the needs and capacity of the library is a vital part of the role of coordinating review and is essential to establishing criteria (like a cost threshold or cost savings measure) that prompt review. Only with a firm grasp of both the time available for review and stakeholders' communication needs can you successfully integrate review processes. Assessment techniques can be as simple as asking questions in your regular meetings, or may take the form of a staff survey at larger libraries. Whatever form the assessment takes, the crucial and central questions those undertaking the review must answer are:

1. Who should be consulted?
2. What are the parameters (budget, content, usage) that should guide decision-making?
3. What time is available for review?
4. What is the correct venue (meeting/asynchronous discussion) for review?
5. What documentation do we want to record about decision-making for future reviewers?
6. Where will we record decisions?
7. How will decisions be communicated to internal and external stakeholders?

ORGANIZING REVIEW DOCUMENTATION

Standardize your review as much as possible, to ensure a data-informed and manageable process. Per earlier discussion, basic review documentation should incorporate the following:

- resource title
- publisher/vendor
- subscription dates
- content description
- cost data
- usage data
- qualitative data
- cancellation clauses in licenses

Suppose you don't have a system already in place for storing this information and keeping track of decisions over time. In that case, you should consider this context when establishing an annual review system. You will need something to track the workflow of the review process (spreadsheet, database, email folders, project management system, etc.) and a well-structured space for storing relevant documentation and decisions for future reference. In general, you will likely end up using several tools to accomplish this, since each library's resources and needs will vary. As of the publication of this book, no one has yet developed a single resource review tool that can handle all these needs for every library type; however, some commonly used tools include spreadsheets, databases, survey software, and visualization software.

Once you have established the standard format for presenting this documentation for stakeholders and decision-makers (see Figures 7.6 and 7.7), you can enrich the reporting format and build off these basic components. For example, if you or your colleagues have implemented reports to track annual usage and cost, tracking rates of increase or decrease in those areas the next year is a natural and practical data point.

Have you seen a cost increase of 5%, while usage declined by 10%? This data, showing the trends of cost increases and usage decreases, will help you have an empowered negotiation with the vendor contact or a candid conversation with the stakeholder advocating for the renewal.

A quick note about qualitative data in the list above: Establishing a simple and standard means of collecting qualitative data on e-resources (which may be as simple as "Professor Xavier needs this e-resource for his research on supporting gifted children") will be crucial to your review documentation and to any ensuing communications. Developing a short survey that you or colleagues send to key stakeholders and that you update at intervals may be all it takes to get this information in a workable format.

Many libraries have bundled e-resources that are lumped into a single renewal; for example, a package of multiple databases with the same subscription start and end dates, or a package of multiple e-journal titles from one publisher. In the review and examination of such packages, it is still useful to parse out individual resources' usage to look for opportunities to make swaps for potentially better content with the vendor. If an entire package is facing declining usage and rising cost, resource-level analysis paired with package-level analysis may become a critical part of your annual review process.

USAGE STATISTICS AND COUNTER REPORTS

The amount we know about how our e-resource collections are used is staggering. While we may grapple with a sense of ambiguity regarding who our online users are, usage reports offer concrete data on what's being used and what's not being used.

In examining usage reports, one critical distinction to be aware of is between COUNTER data and non-COUNTER usage reports. Project COUNTER is a nonprofit organization founded as a collaboration among publishers, vendors, and libraries. COUNTER statistics adhere to COUNTER standards, meaning that resources (and their usage) can be more easily compared. A related reporting schema, SUSHI (Schemas for the Standardized Usage Statistics Harvesting Initiative), can be used to help you quickly collect standard reports from COUNTER-compliant resources.

Figure 7.3
Summary Table of Standard COUNTER Release 4 Reports

Format	Abbreviation	Description
Journal	JR1	Number of successful full-text article requests by month and journal
Journal	JR2	Access denied to full-text articles by month, journal, and category
Journal	JR5	Number of successful full-text article requests by year of publication (YOP) and journal
Database	DB1	Total searches, result clicks, and record views by month and database
Database	DB2	Access denied by month, database, and category
Platform	PR1	Total searches, result clicks, and record views by month and platform
Book	BR1	Number of successful title requests by month and title
Book	BR2	Number of successful section requests by month and title
Book	BR3	Access denied to content items by month, title, and category
Multimedia	MM1	Number of successful full multimedia content unit requests by month and collection

Figure 7.4
Summary Table of Standard COUNTER Release 5 Reports

Format	Abbreviation	Description
Platform	PR_P1	A standard view of the Platform Master Report offering platform-level usage summarized by metric type

Database	DR_D1	Reports on key search, investigation, and request metrics needed to evaluate a database
Database	DR_D2	Reports on activity for databases where users were denied access because simultaneous-use licenses were exceeded or their institution did not have a license for the database
Journal	TR_J1	Reports on usage of non–gold open-access journal content in total and separated out as unique requests that reduce the inflationary effect that occurs when HTML full text automatically displays and then users access the PDF version
Journal	TR_J2	Reports on activity for journal content where users were denied access because simultaneous-use licenses were exceeded or their institution did not have a license for the title
Journal	TR_J4	Breaks down the usage of non–gold open-access journal content by year of publication, providing the details necessary to analyze usage of backfiles content or content covered by perpetual-access agreement
Book	TR_B1	Reports on full-text activity for non–gold open-access books in total and broken down by how the content is delivered (e.g., chapter-level, entry-level)
Book	TR_B2	Reports on activity for books where users were denied access because simultaneous-use licenses were exceeded or their institution did not have a license for the book
Multimedia	IR_M1	Reports on multimedia requests at the item level

Given that COUNTER 5 reporting formats are a recent change, we will still be using COUNTER 4 data for looking at multiyear trends for a while. Since you will likely have historical usage data in COUNTER 4 formats and more contemporary data in COUNTER 5 formats, here is a brief crosswalk to allow you to continue to examine trends in the data.

Figure 7.5
Crosswalk between relevant COUNTER 4 and COUNTER 5 reports

Format	R4	R5 [parameters]
Book	BR1	TR_B1 [Unique_Title_Requests + Data_Type=Book]
Book	BR2	TR_B1 [Total_Item_Requests + Data_Type=Chapter]
Book	BR3	TR_B2 [all]
Journal	JR1	TR_J1 [Unique_Title_Requests + Data_Type=eJournal]
Journal	JR2	TR_J2 [all]
Journal	JR5	TR_J4 [Unique_Item_Requests + Data_Type=eJournal]
Database	DB1	DR_D1 [all]
Database	DB2	DR_D2 [all]
Platform	PR1	PR_P1 [all]
Multimedia	MM1	IR_M1 [all]

Smaller-scale e-resource vendors whose traditional markets are not academic often provide non-COUNTER usage data. While standardized data is easier to work from, and while COUNTER data simplifies work processes, it's important to weigh any inconvenience caused by non-COUNTER usage data against the importance of supporting a diversity of e-resource vendors. Supporting smaller vendors is one means a library can use to help oppose market consolidations and monopolies, which can have devastating effects on the variety and diversity of materials available to our users.

As much as we would like for usage data to be a universal tool, in order to assess resources in an apples-to-apples fashion, the type of resource or the way it is implemented will impact usage reporting in ways that turn it into more of an apples-to-oranges comparison. Database platforms that allow you to search across multiple databases muddy the value of counting searches, particularly for specialized databases lumped in with interdisciplinary databases. In this instance, you might choose to track record views instead.

For resources with mixed access (e.g., an e-book platform for which your institution purchases only select titles or there is a limited number of simultaneous users permitted for select content), the review should include some consideration of access denials, or turnaways, for content not licensed by the library. This might be an indication of an area of your collection that needs development.

If an annual usage report indicates a resource has had zero uses, it's important to have a library staff member test the discoverability and accessibility of the resource. If the resource is currently unreachable through library discovery systems, take steps to correct the access issue. Review any anecdotal evidence of value from stakeholders within the context of other quantitative and qualitative information about use before canceling the resource. In cases of larger e-resource portfolios where access is in place and there is no use, the e-resources manager may want to implement an auto-cancellation process.

LEVERAGING DECISION-MAKING DATA

Publisher-provided usage data following the COUNTER standard does not tell you much more than that an authorized user accessed the material at some point during a month, so it can be difficult to derive additional meaning from the data. To use it to make informed collections decisions, it's best to view it in the aggregate. If the resource is supporting a small academic department with few majors, usage can vary wildly, as relevant classes may not be taught regularly, and it's important to verify that the course is still being taught. You will want to look at several years of data, and it may be helpful to graph the data from multiple years over each other to see if use patterns emerge. Low use for specialized resources may be less concerning than downward-trending use. Historical usage comparisons may be complicated by the adoption of COUNTER release version 5, as there are some significant changes in how usage is reported. You should keep this in mind when determining which metric is most appropriate for that resource.

Resources from publishers that aren't primarily focused on the academic market will likely not have usage data in the COUNTER standard. This is frustrating when you want to compare two similar resources, but if they provide any usage data, this can still be helpful in making renewal decisions if the data provided remains consistent from year to year and has some indication of the value of the content. For example, the number of reports downloaded from a business database is a useful metric, but the number of webpage views recorded by the server isn't useful.

Another data point to monitor over several years is the price paid for the resource and the percentage by which it increased (or decreased) each year. This can be a useful predictor of the renewal price, if you don't yet have that information from the publisher, and can also play a role in your decision if it appears that the trend for increases is unsustainable. For example, a library budget may be able to absorb a 6% annual increase for a long time on a low-cost resource, but for resources costing hundreds of thousands of dollars, you might need to start planning an exit strategy.

In addition, it's useful to track the often-shifting content within a resource:

- Has it stayed constant?
- Has the vendor/publisher added new content?
- Has the vendor/publisher removed content?

It's challenging to monitor such changes, and it will require engagement with vendor representatives and clear communication with stakeholders. In general, content analysis is more time consuming than asking a good question of a vendor representative, though getting clear answers may also take time. Leaning on vendor infrastructures and staff is a best practice, particularly for those operating with limited staff resources of their own.

USEFUL EXCEL FUNCTIONS

If it isn't apparent from the sections regarding data above, much of the work of resource review will be done in spreadsheets. Using Microsoft Excel to make this work easier can allow for time to be refocused on the important and time-sensitive work of communicating findings and decisions.

Figure 7.6
Excel Functions for Resource Review

Excel Function	What It Does	When It Is Useful
COUNTIF	Counts number of cells that meet a specified criterion	Content analysis
COUNTBLANK	Counts blanks (missing data)	Identifying missing/blank fields
SUM	Adds values to a total	Cost analysis
VLOOKUP	Links data from a different table or range	Combining data from multiple spreadsheets/ tabs
Conditional Formatting	Applies formatting to cells that meet a specified criterion	At-a-glance visualization and analysis

Examining title lists and coverage lists may become a critical part of e-resource review, providing an opportunity to identify duplicative content and recoup budget. Using COUNTIF to find matching titles, combined with conditional formatting to provide an easy visual highlight of those titles, may be a simple tool to help start some conversations about content.

VLOOKUP is helpful for working with multiple data sources. For example, if you are looking at journal subscriptions, you can use VLOOKUP to combine usage data from one source with cost data from another source, provided both contain the ISSN or other match point. IF statements combined with VLOOKUP can be useful for filling in unmatched lines with a text or numeric default.

Figure 7.7
Excel Chart Example

Calendar Year	YOP Pre-2012	YOP 2012	YOP 2013	YOP 2014	YOP 2015	YOP 2016	YOP 2017	YOP 2018
2012	889	248	2					
2013	5860	1260	1857	2				
2014	5119	700	1514	1696	1			
2015	5155	796	857	1323	1420			
2016	4309	746	943	1068	1621	2058	5	
2017	4515	729	1165	1258	1227	2283	2496	4

Visualizations of data are very helpful for decision-makers who aren't familiar with interpreting tabular data. Excel graphs do provide some rough tools for those visualizations, but by making some adjustments to the formatting, you can highlight the important data stories hidden in the graphs.

For example, Figure 7.7 shows usage compiled from several years of JR5 reports (COUNTER 4), starting in calendar year 2012. You could break down the back-issue usage even further by year, but combining those years simplifies and highlights backfile versus frontfile usage.

Figure 7.8 is the default stacked graph generated by Excel based on the data in Figure 7.7—confusing and not particularly useful. After a few tweaks, you will have something that tells a story about this journal collection and how it is being used by students and faculty.

We created Figure 7.9 after switching the column and row data, adjusting the labels, adding a title, adjusting the gap width, adjusting the font size and weight, and adding and formatting data labels to replace the legend. You could do more, but this begins to tell a data story that decision-makers will understand more clearly: Usage is increasing over time, and the portion of the usage coming from the current or previous year of publication is also increasing. This indicates that the collection has value not only for the currently published research, but also research published in the recent past that might now be getting cited in more recent publications.

Figure 7.8
Excel Stacked Graph Example—Default

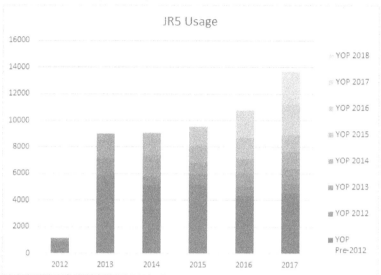

As you refine the process of resource review, developing a competency around interactions with the data becomes a critical part of the work, essential to the success of the resource review and the e-resources collection.

FACILITATING STAKEHOLDER INVOLVEMENT

If your budget can sustain maintaining for an additional year a subscription that you're considering for cancellation, you have a good opportunity to spend some time engaging with stakeholders before you pull the plug. It may be that the faculty member who used it most retired and their replacement isn't familiar with the resource, and an email or hallway chat could prompt them to consider it for their research or teaching. If a library staff member is giving an instruction session on topics covered by the resource, they can be sure to include it so that students are aware of the value of the resource for their assignments.

Figure 7.9
Excel Stacked Graph Example—Modified
Note: YOP = Year of Purchase and CY = Calendar Year

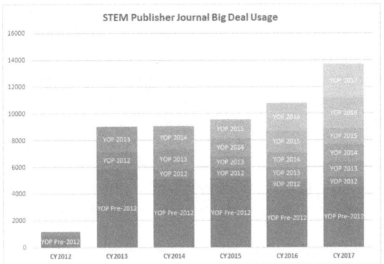

You will benefit from engaging with the full library outreach team to facilitate productive conversations about the collection and e-resource decision-making. Sharing data and processes, and providing opportunities for feedback and input, all help to improve both relationships and the collection.

If your community has digital signage, email announcements, or other means for broadly communicating with students and faculty, this is another opportunity to raise awareness about the resource. If, after all this, you still don't see an increase in engagement with the resource, then you can confidently remove it from your collection.

VENDOR COMMUNICATIONS

As previously mentioned when we discussed leveraging decision-maker data, communication with vendors is a critical part of the e-resource review process. As the renewal date for an e-resource approaches, you should engage with your vendor contact to ensure that you have access to the most up-to-date pricing and usage information, as well as notify the vendor if the library is taking a close look at a given e-resource. This professional courtesy and communication will help create smooth transitions where necessary and offer opportunities to explore renegotiation in cases that merit it. Good relationships with vendor representatives make the work of e-resource review simpler and less time consuming.

Vendor communication can be a factor in e-resource review. File your email exchanges and make notes on phone calls throughout the year, keeping these in some place where you can easily search and retrieve them. If you think these details are significant enough to be relevant to decision-makers, be sure to include them along with other data points in your review.

In some instances, anomalies in usage identified in the e-resource review may unearth access issues or account setup issues that will require coordination with the vendor's support team to resolve. Maintaining good business relations can usually lead to a smoother resolution.

CONTEXTUALIZING THE COMMUNITY

Beyond the on-hand data of cost and usage, it's important for library colleagues to have a broader view of renewing e-resources in the context of the institution and/or served communities. One essential objective of e-resource review must be this contextualization, which may prove a slippery process but is worth undertaking. This process can be informal or formal, but should involve at minimum a cursory review of:

- **community strategy and priority documents**: For example, is institutional administration pushing for data science initiatives? What should collections support look like?
- **new majors and/or programs added each year**: For example, if

your institution introduces an American Studies program, are current holdings in American history sufficient? Or, if your community is focusing on makerspaces for high school students, do you have library resources to support that?

- **majors and/or programs eliminated in a year**: For example, if your institution is no longer teaching philosophy, should you continue to subscribe to philosophy resources?
- **accreditation:** For example, is a specific e-resource required for a major's accredidation?

This contextualization step provides important input to any decision to renew or cancel an e-resource, and often necessitates outreach engagement with faculty, allowing for selectors to deepen relationships and develop a deeper understanding of their collections as they support research and learning. Ultimately, whatever the decision, this review process can help provide important rationale documentation, which benefits the rigor of a resource review process.

REMEMBERING THE BIG PICTURE

Another piece of resource decision-making that can be overlooked due to the crush of the budget cycle is the broader question of the implications of what we buy, whom we buy it from, and who has access. In our rush to ensure access to content to meet community needs, we may miss opportunities to have conversations about the sustainability of serials, for instance, and the social justice opportunities of the "open" movement (e.g., open-access publishing and open educational resources). By beginning to have these conversations with community stakeholders, e-resources staff and selectors will demonstrate awareness of the revolution in scholarly communication and publishing. It also presents the opportunity for more proactive e-resource decision-making. If libraries are going to be effective leaders of a new era of scholarly communication, it begins with these interactions.

Developing a sense of the big picture for a subject area will require a developed and nuanced understanding. Being able to communicate that with stakeholders will prove invaluable. Some questions to consider at the beginning of the budget cycle:

1. How do our vendor partners support sustainable scholarship?
2. How does our e-resources collection support scholarship from under-represented communities and researchers of color?
3. Should we renew this resource directly with the vendor or are there consortial/group deal opportunities?
4. How are we planning ahead to address ongoing inflation? How are we future-proofing critical e-resources collections?
5. What proportion of our budget can we allocate to support open scholarship? What open access projects make sense for our users?
6. Does the materials budget allow for the library to explore options for publishing?

In many ways, any collections position is a dual steward—of the existing collection and of the ongoing budget. By keeping the big picture in mind, and interrogating the budget and collection practices regularly, you enhance your library's e-resource review process.

MAKING AN INFORMED CHOICE

E-resource decision-making can feel high stakes, but if you have incorporated data and communicated with stakeholders and vendors to develop a systematic resource review process, you and your colleagues can have the confidence of knowing that, together, you are making an informed choice. Simplifying and presenting the data, standardizing reporting and the review process—all these critical steps of a resource review establish and maintain a responsive, defensible, and agile e-resources collection. Resource review is a valuable strategic tool in the process of e-resources management.

CITATIONS AND FURTHER READING

Emery, A. K. (2014, July 9). =vlookup(): One Excel function to rule them all. *Depict Data Studio.* https://annkemery.com/vlookup/

Emery, A. K. (2016, October 27). The data visualization checklist, 2016 edition. *Depict Data Studio.* https://annkemery.com/checklist/

Emery, A. K. (2017, July 18). How to transform a table of data into a chart: Four charts with four different stories. *Depict Data Studio.* https://depictdatastudio.com/how-to -transform-a-table-of-data-into-a-chart-four-charts-with-four-different-stories/

Emery, J., & Stone, G. (2013). *Techniques for electronic resource management.* Chicago: ALA TechSource. https://doi.org/10.5860/ltr.49n2

Kennedy, M. R., & LaGuardia, C. (2018). *Marketing your library's electronic resources: A how-to-do-it manual for librarians* (2nd ed.). ALA Neal-Schuman.

National Information Standards Association. (2014). *Standardized Usage Statistics Harvesting Initiative (SUSHI) protocol (ANSI/NISO Z39.93-2014).* https://www.niso.org /standards-committees/sushi

Project COUNTER. (n.d.). 4.0 COUNTER reports. *The COUNTER Code of Practice for Release 5.* https://www.projectcounter.org/code-of-practice-five-sections/4-1-usage- reports/

Project COUNTER (2021). Friendly guides and manual for librarians. *Project COUNTER.* https://www.projectcounter.org/friendly-guides-release-5/

Verminski, A., & Blanchat, K. M. (2017). *Fundamentals of electronic resources management.* ALA Neal-Schuman.

Eight

Cancellation and Replacement

Erika Ripley and Scarlet Galvan

There are many reasons for the library to embark on a cancellation project: rising subscription costs, new leadership, external mandates, vendors not meeting a licensing need, an unexpected funding shortfall. Regardless of the precipitating event, the library is about to manage a significant and time-intensive project that can last several years. We have both encountered cancellations of various sizes and scope throughout our careers, as observers and direct participants in the process.

We first wish to offer context for this chapter. As of this writing, we both have backgrounds in academic libraries, including institutions categorized by the Carnegie Classification of Institutions of Higher Education as Research I Universities (R1s), selective baccalaureate colleges (SLACs), and health sciences library environments. We have done our best to address the limits of our experiences, when possible, to make this chapter flexible. Each library is unique in its staffing, structure, funding models, political challenges, and overall culture. These variables have tremendous influence on any library project and its ultimate outcome. We both believe opportunity is inherent to the cancellation process. We haven't directly addressed short-term or one-off title cancellations, as everyday workflows between libraries will vary. While Chapter 7 focuses on establishing regular reviews that may lead to a cancellation, this chapter focuses on cancellation projects beyond the scope of a single title or database, and beyond regular maintenance of the collection. If your library asks you to break a package or Big Deal, we wrote this for you.

We chose to write this chapter for many reasons, but the most important are:

- our belief in the library as an authority on its own collection decisions
- the library as facilitator for difficult but active and engaged conversations with its users

MYTHS AND LEGENDS

Libraries often invoke feelings of nostalgia and mythologies from those who don't work in them about what a library "should" be (Carr, 2015; Seeber, 2018; Zahneis, 2018). These narratives involve personal stories that are valuable when considering political implications of cancellation. Communication strategies and evaluation criteria used during large weeding projects may be helpful to redeploy during cancellation. See, for example, McAllister and Scherlen's (2017) thorough discussion of faculty response to routine collection maintenance, in particular outreach opportunities created during a well-managed feedback process: "Although the quantity of books saved by faculty review was not significantly large, the library benefited by identifying important titles, reducing concerns on campus about the project, and creating new relationships between librarians and faculty who had not been engaged with the library in the past."

A healthy cancellation process should reflect knowledge about the collection gleaned from a variety of sources, if for no other reason than that the acquisition of this knowledge should be a regular practice for a responsive collection. The library can refine the process the library chooses to implement depending on the nature of the process or size of the cut.

No library can hold everything, and it's unreasonable to frame discussion of cancellation at any level around whether or not a particular resource is essential, beyond a strict accreditation requirement. Cancellation does, however, provide unparalleled opportunities for realignment, to build and refine an engaging collection that is responsive, useful, and co-created to serve both users and library workers. Research interests, curriculum, disciplinary trends, communities, and strategic initiatives that shape a library will be reflected in what gets used and requested. Cancellations can foster stronger resource sharing networks and consortia relationships, better user understanding of library services, favorable licensing terms on retained contracts, and can situate the library as more than "the stuff" but as genuine collaborators and partners.

CRITERIA AND RATIONALE

Planning is foundational. The actual execution of a library-wide project with huge impact will be vastly more successful due to the library's thoughtful consideration of what will need to happen, when, and by whom, in advance.

Simon Fraser's model of a representational working group is functional at universities where the institution and library's stakeholders see the library as a trusted expert in the situation, because it centers the library as authoritative about the collection while acknowledging stakeholder interests through shared governance (Simon Fraser University Library, 2015).

Florida State University Libraries' move to end its Big Deal with Elsevier appears quite successful, in part due to extensive outreach from the library to FSU's faculty governance about the nature of the collection, the opaque nature of the pricing structure offered to FSU, and the failure of Elsevier to offer a sustainable alternative (Elsevier Subscription Changes, 2020). The university shared the decisions, which served to communicate that they were not made by the library acting alone or without adequate support for their decision. The same is true of the University of California system's Elsevier exit, a multi institution effort of almost 20 years.

Brandon Butler and John Unsworth's excellent work at the University of Virginia Libraries is another example of engaging this task in fruitful ways that center the library as an authority, rather than abdicating responsibility for the maintenance of the collection to faculty (Butler and Unsworth, 2018). We realize all libraries attempt to consider their stakeholders when making significant cuts, but waiting too long for decisions or not promoting shared governance over those choices hurts the library on every front. Waiting on feedback without considering your original timeline, or without creating a timeline that allows your stakeholders to have a meaningful voice, results in deteriorated vendor relationships, upset users, and technical services staff scrambling to compensate for last-minute decisions with massive systems implications.

Library staff with the variety of expertise necessary for the project must come into the process as early as possible. It can be helpful to think of this expertise broadly, from project management and data analysis to marketing and outreach. Depending on the size of your library, this all may fall squarely within the duties of one person. Larger libraries must involve technical services, resource management, communication and marketing staff, and fiscal officers first, in order to avoid creating panic among primarily user-facing staff. Alienating staff with expertise to help with collection analysis and strategic cancellation is problematic and can result in embarrassment for the library later on. Don't make cuts in a vacuum. See, for example, Chapter 6, on completing ongoing evaluation and systematic access checks, and Chapter 7, on annual reviews of e-resource collections.

COMMUNICATING

Communication is critical to preserving both internal and external relationships in order to reach the best possible outcome in a cancellation project. External stakeholders will all want to hear factual information from you about cancellations as early as is reasonable. The examples we have chosen to illustrate successfully executed cancellation projects all have foundations in defined roles, data transparency, and clear communication.

Communication is integral to the workflow, timeline, and infrastructure surrounding the work that will hold a cancellation project together. We're highlighting it here because it's important, not because it's a distinct process. After the project ends, the library will continue to engage with users about its collection, services, and staff expertise. Cancellations are difficult and often unpopular work, but successful communication can build partnerships between the library and community.

Libraries can collaborate with their agents, consortia, and vendors throughout a cancellation. Libraries should undertake this collaboration thoughtfully and strategically. There are aspects of communicating these projects unique to each third-party stakeholder. We offer some considerations below:

Publishers and Content Providers

- Even if the library is breaking a Big Deal, it may be possible to negotiate terms for the individual subscriptions it will maintain or for a different package that meets local needs. The library will need to engage with the vendor early enough to allow time for those discussions. Many third-party providers will ask for in-person meetings when feasible if an institution announces a cancellation.
- Even if the library is certain about cancellation as the only possible outcome and will not be considering renewal, e-resources staff will very likely need information from publishers on other package options, price quotes for individual subscriptions, and entitlement confirmation reports for post-cancellation access. Yes, the publisher or provider is disappointed that the library is cancelling, and negotiations that led up to the cancellation decision may have strained the relation-

ship, but maintaining a strong working relationship is worthwhile. Cancelling a package does not mean never dealing with a particular vendor again.

- Some vendors may choose to contact library users directly during negotiations, and libraries should prepare for this possibility.
- Be up front about the library's timeline for decision-making and budget constraints.
- Alert them as early as is practical that cancellation is a possibility receiving serious consideration.

Subscription Agents

- Cancellations may have an impact on the library's subscription agent service fees. Service fees are negotiable, but the library will need to engage with agents early, to facilitate planning and to allow time for discussion.
- Library cancellations are likely to reduce the agents' bottom lines, so they are eager to know as soon as possible that the library is anticipating cancellations.
- E-resources staff need to understand how cancellation may impact renewal or ordering workflows.
- Subscription agents may need new or updated information (e.g., in a package breakup, they may need new fund instructions and ILS numbers for any titles the library retains).
- Subscription agents often carry journal packages and databases on different accounts from individual subscriptions. Renewing individual journals often requires a workflow with an agent that differs from renewing a package. Be sure to consider how much additional labor this may create, in order to build in time and allocate staff to implement any changes.

Consortium Partners

- If a consortium offers the resource the library is cancelling, be sure consortium staff or partners are aware of the library's plans to withdraw. One library's cancellation may impact their deal, packages, or available pricing for the next cycle.
- Sometimes the total number of participants in a deal is a factor in the discounts available to all participants.
- Determine if there are consortial offers the library previously did not pursue that it should consider now.

Internal Communications

We stress avoiding duplication of effort throughout this chapter because it is critical. In the absence of a communication plan, library staff and users may rely on alternative narratives, often creating unintentional rumors. This takes valuable time away from communicating facts and forces the library to address assumptions instead of relationship building.

All Project Team Members

- Use calendar scheduling to defensively block off time for work on the cancellation.
- Establish a regular communication schedule for project updates and milestones, even if the update is just "the library is continuing negotiations" or "we have an updated timeline."
- Determine who will communicate updates to which audience (University of California, 2019).

Technical Services

- Check in regularly to prevent duplication of effort.
- Schedule recurring regular meetings. They can be canceled if not needed, but hold space for them.

- Determine how you are dividing up work (e.g., by publisher/package/title/workflow).
- Determine who is doing what steps and in what order.
- Have open meetings for those not directly involved with the project to receive updates and offer suggestions.

Public Services/Subject Specialists/Instructional Services

- Users may contact the staff they identify most as "the library" because of the working relationships established. Anyone staffing a service desk may receive questions or complaints from users.
- At minimum, library staff should be able to direct users to a website or statement that discusses the project.
- Library workers with reference duties, instructional responsibilities, or subject expertise are often sounding boards for feedback about the collection from users. Make sure they can communicate such feedback to the project team.
- Cancellations can build on user-facing relationships, and having the library's most visible staff say "I don't know" is a lost opportunity for the library to center that staff member's expertise and authority.

Interlibrary Loan/Resource Sharing

- If your resource sharing infrastructure is dependent on ILL rights statements in knowledgebases, package and Big Deal breakups will alter resource sharing workflows in both lending and borrowing.
- Resource sharing staff may be responsible for maintaining accurate holdings in union lists or cooperative catalogs and will need details on cancellations to update those systems.
- Many resource sharing staff see changes in the collection as a research opportunity to study changes in ILL activity patterns, the volume of requests, and copyright fees. Providing information about

what the library canceled will allow this analysis and development to move forward.

CONSIDERING THE COMMUNITY

Creating expectations about what the library will maintain can be risky, especially when the library has different ideas about how the collection serves the community versus other stakeholders, or when internal perspectives of library staff differ. Cancellations offer fantastic opportunities for the library to meaningfully redefine what the role of the collection is, in service to the community, and for the library staff to create or build internal collaborative relationships. Ideally, the library is either a known authority on the collection or can use a cancellation project to move toward that status.

Avoid guaranteeing resource access or communicating with language that suggests a promise. Doing so creates problems for any library, but in particular affects:

- libraries with precarious staffing arrangements (e.g., temporary or contract staff, or over-reliance on part-time lines or volunteers to provide essential services)
- libraries without identifiable leadership. This takes a variety of forms but is exacerbated when the library is positioned exclusively as a provider of content and services, not as an institutional partner with authority over the collection.
- solo library staff in corporate or special library environments

Not even the most well-resourced institutions in the world expect to maintain a "comprehensive" collection (Linden et al., 2018). The library must carefully frame budget issues as far away from staffing lines as possible. Gather allies among your users to speak to the value of services, generally speaking, and not a specific database or product. Advocate for service over content whenever possible. Budget realities change, as do

user priorities. Getting a resource back is trivial compared to restoring a
job line.

Publishers and content providers are responsible for creating a landscape where increases that far exceed inflation are common. Libraries
confident enough to do so can shift this discussion to a shared governance
model, agree to reject large increases, and stop devaluing their own labor
by performing free work for publishers.

ESTABLISHING ROLES/PROJECT PLANNING

Cancellation projects are different enough from other types of resource reviews that internal discussion of the project goal, roles, and
responsibilities should be a part of the up-front planning. These projects can engage staff and invested stakeholders from across the library
and beyond. All active project participants should have a shared understanding of the goals, timelines, and parameters within which they
will be working.

Both internal and external deadlines will be obvious and critical dri-
vers of the work of any cancellation project. When does the library make a
decision within the library? Budget cycles and resource subscription terms
will inform decisions and timelines, but planners should also be mindful of how the timing of any resultant cancellations will impact users.
For academic libraries, the ends of calendar and fiscal years tend to cor-
respond to breaks between class sessions. In addition to contractual and
budgetary deadlines, consider what other important dates impact your
users. For example, medical school library staff might avoid announcing
cuts to biomedical journals and databases on Match Day, a major annual
event. Calendaring out what is important to your users should be part of
setting the overall project timeline.

Roles and responsibilities will need to be clarified at the project outset. Some examples of questions to ask as early as possible are:

- Who are the project decision-makers?
- Which departments and/or staff are compiling data for decision-making?
- Questions about costs, savings, inflation, and budgets are very likely to be intertwined with the work of a cancellation project. Who can and should be providing the details needed to answer those questions as they arise? As mentioned in the section of this chapter entitled "Ongoing Evaluation," core library systems are often controlled by outside units.
- Who is responsible for which deliverables?
- If the cancellation attracts media coverage or wide discussion in the community, how should the library respond, and who is responsible for doing so?
- How much time are you willing to allow for feedback from stakeholders?

Staff compiling project data may need to engage with colleagues in other areas for custom reports or raw data. Staff compiling data may collaborate with coworkers with expertise in data visualization or analysis to prepare reports. Clarifying functional roles as well as project goals up front will help reduce confusion as unexpected issues come up during the project, prevent duplication of work and overlooking tasks, and allow library staff to put into place the processes necessary to support them in their work. Libraries may want to consider using some project management principles to facilitate internal planning and discussions, such as a project charter. A charter can be a very useful tool in planning and talking through how the various aspects of a complex project fit together. We include a sample project plan in Appendix A.

IDENTIFYING WHAT DATA POINTS TO COLLECT

There are many motivators behind the library taking up a cancellation project. A library's context-specific situation should inform what data inputs are collected and what evaluation processes are put in place. Chapter 7, Getting Started with Resource Review, offers a solid foundation on the data sources useful for resource evaluation and assessment. Appendix B, following this chapter, also provides a sample list of the types of data sources to consider. In the context of a cancellation project, library staff should consider the goal of the project as well as who the project stakeholders and decision makers are when defining the scope of the data to compile, analyze, and present. Doing so will help make certain that the gathered data meets the assessment needs of the library's particular situation and goals.

For instance, if a Big Deal is highlighted for potential cancellation due to high cost, the library may also consider data about other access points to the content, or external data about the user population most impacted by the cancellation. Does an aggregator database also in the collection constitute an acceptable source of alternative access to key journals if the library cancels that Big Deal package? How large is the primary group of users for the titles being canceled? What percentage of titles in the package are open access? The broader context of the cancellation under consideration should shape and inform the project's data compilation.

Usage data are often the cornerstone of resource assessment. Chapter 7 offers a detailed discussion of COUNTER and non-COUNTER usage reports, and makes the critical point that it can be difficult to divine meaning from this data. In a cancellation review, usage data cannot stand on its own, distinct from context, nor does it present a complete picture of usage or the needs of users. For example, usage reports can be overwhelming at an institution with high research activity, where scholars may access dozens of articles during their research but only cite a handful, and publish their outputs in still fewer venues. Libraries of all types and sizes serve a multitude of subsets within the overall user community. What does usage for a product of broad interest look like, compared to usage for a product with a narrower focus? How will usage be interpreted alongside data on cost or user demographics, or an assessment of the resource's quality, usability, and discoverability? If the library is struggling to decide what data is important to include and evaluate, consider reviewing the organizational strategic plan or the overall goal for the cancellation project for guidance.

Measures like altmetrics, usage data, circulation statistics, impact factor, and community input each serve as a separate data point when evaluating resources. Each of these metrics, when considered independently, are too easily generalized into a superficial understanding of a resource's value. Understanding long-term patterns is important and often requires pulling multiple years of data to see how use changes with events, new programs and initiatives, or changes in hiring. One e-resources management specialist saw use of a disciplinary resource's backfile triple in a single year, only to discover the increase was driven by faculty members on sabbatical. Usage data only tells part of the story. Impact factor should not be applied to articles or authors, but rather can describe the overall performance of one journal. Altmetrics can rapidly shift if a group of new users are active on social media.

If you're going to consider external measures like altmetrics or impact factor, these will require technical expertise, staff time, and institutional resources to manage. Appeals to metrics should be handled carefully and be dependent on the needs of the population the library serves.

Packages of resources, databases, and Big Deals present some specific data compilation challenges for evaluation. When packages and databases are being reviewed for potential cancellation, data will be obtained from a variety of sources, potentially including the ILS, the ERMS, other core library systems (e.g., EZProxy, OpenURL resolvers), the publisher, and subscription agents. Files from these disparate sources are going to include different data points and will reflect variations on resource or journal titles. Package title lists from different sources will likely represent combination orders or bundled titles differently and they may or may not include elements like institution-specific costs, list prices, and consistent, standard numbers. Some amount of data cleanup or normalization is usually necessary to combine data points into a single file, spreadsheet, or report for evaluators.

Staff compiling files for review may want to highlight particular title characteristics for the attention of stakeholders or evaluators, such as which titles are open access or are included in bundles. In a Big Deal evaluation, evaluators will need title-level pricing for both historically subscribed titles and those titles available as part of the Big Deal collection, as well as ILL costs for articles from unsubscribed journals. The publisher may not make applicable list prices public, or title-level pricing may not yet be available at the time of review. Libraries using the most current list price available in evaluations should allow for some flexibility, since they may be making cancellation decisions for the following subscription year. Most packages have capped, predictable inflation rates specified as part of a multiyear agreement. Decision-makers will need information on the financial impacts of breaking a package beyond ordering journals individually, such as higher and less predictable inflation going forward.

FILE HYGIENE

Library staff will create, revise, exchange, and share numerous library files during any cancellation project. While file hygiene and documentation are always important, they can be critical in the midst of this cancellation work. Data compilers, analyzers, evaluators, and decision-makers will all benefit from having clarity around how information will be created, stored, and exchanged. Taking time to organize and plan for the specific challenges of moving work around internally can prevent confusion later and make the processing of cancellation decisions easier. Consider choosing or generating a unique identifier to use in all project files. Doing so will facilitate combining data from various sources, reuniting files or elements that have been separated, and tying all relevant data together for staff who will need to act on decisions. Further suggestions for data considerations are in Appendix B.

Many libraries make use of various project management or productivity tools and software such as Microsoft OneNote or Planner, Trello, Airtable, or Slack. A part of the planning should include identifying and documenting how and where staff working on the project will keep meeting notes, task lists, data files, and reports. Whether the library elects to use such a tool or other local file storage spaces, staff should be consistent in their practices. Having a predictable location for project materials will prevent stray pieces being overlooked in various file spaces. Consider and make decisions on the following:

- file-naming protocol
- file-editing etiquette and mechanisms to track changes
- file storage space and backup
- methods for tracking progress on tasks from start to completion

Having these decisions made at the outset will support staff who are working with these files during the project, but also afterwards, as the files become a record for decisions made and work done during the cancellation review for both historical and evaluation purposes. Staff working on future cancellation projects can draw on this work to see what was done and how, instead of starting from scratch or relying on fragmented institutional memory.

Given all the data points and files, cancellation projects involve many moving parts. Several different elements of the work will need to be underway simultaneously. Staff could be pulling list prices and historical prices paid for journals in a Big Deal package while also retrieving usage data, mapping titles to locally relevant subjects, or checking into perpetual access rights. Progress on specific tasks or portions of the work will bottleneck at various points as e-resources staff await information from other parties or need to attend to other work.

Staff need to be able to return to the project work, picking back up where they left off; otherwise, it's too easy for steps to be overlooked or for nearly finished work to be stranded as incomplete. Even in small libraries or in projects involving few participants, it's worth breaking down all the work that needs doing into the smallest actionable unit, to track the project and ensure all tasks are completed. In larger libraries, breaking down the work into the smallest actionable units can also facilitate mapping elements of work to various staff as well as ensuring that nothing falls through the cracks.

Clear file hygiene and tracking of work will also prove invaluable if cancellation project decisions are revisited and when project outcomes are evaluated. Say the library planned to cancel *Journal of Z*, but a professor made a strong argument for it and endowment funds were found to reinstate it. Such a hypothetical case prompts the following questions:

- How will e-resources management staff note reinstatements or requests for reinstatement?
- Will questions emerge about how many titles were reinstated after initially being canceled?
- Which library staff will be responsible for answering those questions?

Consider a standard note in ILS records or other project management systems to enable e-resources staff to report on cancellation questions of various kinds or to identify titles part of the project.

Once cancellation decisions are made, the work pivots from internal evaluation to communicating externally and processing the decisions.

POST-CANCELLATION ACCESS

Cancellations may require the library to invoke post-cancellation or perpetual access rights to purchased content. This can take many forms, depending on the type of resource(s) being canceled and the manner of delivery of perpetual access to which the library is entitled. E-resources procedures for acquiring and managing content should include documenting the library's rights to perpetual access; those procedures will be locally driven by the size of the staff, the size of the collection, the ILS or ERMS in use, and related acquisitions workflows. Documenting post-cancellation access rights as an essential project task could take the form of notes on order records, coding in an ERMS, or simply having the details noted in the license agreements. If post-cancellation access rights aren't clearly documented at a granular level when that information is needed for cancellations or if those details aren't available in a readily accessible format, staff will need to investigate what information sources are available to document the years of content to which the library has access. Drawing on information available from multiple sources can help paint the fullest possible picture of access rights. That complete picture will be critical if the library needs to prove its rights to the content provider.

Publishers, content providers, platforms, and subscription agents can produce entitlement reports to supplement or complement perpetual access information available in house. These outside partners may be limited in how many years back their sales records extend, and library subscription histories may go beyond those records. As noted above in the case of title lists, files provided by varying information partners will have different unique identifiers, standard numbers, and title variations. Regardless of the tool used to combine and analyze these files as a cohesive whole, doing so will require some data normalization and clean-up.

Post-cancellation access can look like a lot of different things, so the specifics attached to a particular product cancellation will vary. Will the publisher continue to host content? Are fees involved? The diversity of ways that post-cancellation and archival access might present themselves are beyond the scope of this general chapter, but consider what is known locally about the library's rights and what documentation sources could be drawn on when collecting data for cancellation evaluation. Once e-resources management staff have compiled a picture of the perpetual access rights the library retains, they will need to confirm those rights with the publisher as well as update knowledgebases and other core library systems to indicate the content still available to users following the cancellation. As with all elements of cancellation projects, some consideration for how this work will be organized and tracked while in progress is well worth the time. Depending on the nature of the resource or resources canceled, these updates can involve touching large numbers of titles in multiple systems.

E-resources management staff should also build on their experience of investigating and documenting their perpetual access rights by revisiting workflows for new acquisitions or licensing. How should these rights be documented locally at time of acquisition in order to be easily drawn upon when needed for an evaluation or cancellation? Cancellations will most often be communicated prior to the end of the subscription period, so e-resources staff should also plan to confirm proactively that actual access details match up with expected access once the cancellation has taken effect.

FINAL RECOMMENDATIONS

Strategize for multiple outcomes, especially if there are high levels of uncertainty around funding. This might look like a "worst-case scenario," as opposed to the outcome the library will lobby towards. Remember too, that vendor representatives can and do assist with this because their relationships with you still matter to them.

Under the best conditions, the successful cancellation is driven by pre-existing frameworks, strategies, and relationships. Cancellations will highlight strong processes and relationships and exacerbate strained ones. The work of resource management in libraries is invisible, and yet, when asked how the library can help, academic library users identify resource access as the library's primary responsibility (Smith, 2020). As both authors work through analysis and difficult decisions made explicit by the

COVID-19 pandemic in our own libraries, we also recognize these conversations were overdue throughout the profession, and that many current models of acquisition and delivery are unsustainable. We believe the library, broadly conceived, is more than storage, metrics, and objects, but is a space for advocacy, connection, and the opportunity to imagine shared, sustainable futures.

CITATIONS AND FURTHER READING

Anderson, I. et al., (2019). Negotiating with scholarly journal publishers: A toolkit from the University of California.

Unsworth, J. and Butler, B. Research Information Costs at the University of Virginia, Presentation to the UVA Faculty Senate, Oct. 30, 2018. https://doi.org/10.18130/v3-e8r1-qp62

Carr, P. L. (2015). Serendipity in the stacks: Libraries, information architecture, and the problems of accidental discovery. *College & Research Libraries*, 76(6), 831–842. https://doi.org/10.5860/crl.76.6.831

Florida State University Libraries: Elsevier Subscription Changes (2020). https://www.lib.fsu.edu/elsevier-changes

Hardy, B. B., Zimmerman, M. C., and Hanscom, L. A.. (2016). Cutting without cursing: A successful cancellation project. *The Serials Librarian, 71*(2), 112–120. https://doi.org/10.1080/0361526X.2016.1196635

Linden, J., Tudesco, S., & Dollar, D. (2018). Collections as a service: A research library's perspective. *College & Research Libraries, 79*(1), 86–99. https://doi.org/10.5860/crl.79.1.86

McAllister, A. D., & Scherlen, A. (2017). Weeding with wisdom: Tuning deselection of print monographs in book-reliant disciplines. *Collection Management 42*(2), 76–91. https://libres.uncg.edu/ir/asu/f/McAllister_Scherlen_Weeding_2017_archive.pdf

Seeber, K. (2018, June 15). Legacy systems. *Blog.* http://kevinseeber.com/blog/legacy-systems/

Scholarly Publishing and Academic Resources Coalition (2021) Strategies for Effectively Engaging Stakeholders in Negotiation. https://sparcopen.org/our-work/negotiation-resources/strategies-for-effectively-engaging-stakeholders-in-negotiations/

Simon Fraser University Library: Background: Collections cost reduction (2015) https://www.lib.sfu.ca/about/overview/collections/materials-budget/cost-reduction-2015

Smith, C. (2020, May 28). *Report on the University of Michigan Library's COVID-19 campus survey.* University of Michigan Library. https://deepblue.lib.umich.edu/handle/2027.42/155436

Zahneis, Megan. (2018, June 17). UVa Library's plan to Cut stacks by half sparks faculty concerns. *Chronicle of Higher Education.* https://www.chronicle.com/article/UVa-Library-s-Plan-to-Cut/243610/

APPENDIX A: SAMPLE CANCELLATION PROJECT PLAN AND TIMELINE

Project Description:

(What is the context for the project? What is happening and why?)

The library budget has been flat for several years, and inflation has continued to rise. The overall budget cannot cover the library's current collection of continuing subscriptions without making cancellations or re-allocating money from other sources. In preparation for the next budget year and at the behest of the library director, several areas of collection spending will be reviewed in order to identify potential cancellations. The budget for monographs and other one-time purchases will be reviewed as a separate project in the following budget cycle.

Goals:

(Goals should be concrete and specific.)

- Review all database subscriptions with an annual cost of over $1,000
  - Limit to those with single-year terms or with multiyear terms currently ending this fiscal year
- Identify three cancellation scenarios that would reduce total spending on databases by 10%

Project Team:

(Who is working on the project and in what capacity?)

Project Role	Colleague(s)
Executive sponsor *(initiated the project, ultimate decision-maker)*	Library director
Project sponsor *(in-house champion, able to clear roadblocks or provide resources)*	Assistant director for collections

Project manager *(oversees the hands-on work of the project team, responsible for adherence to timelines and deliverables)*	Head of technical services
Project team members *(actual doers of the project work, may be involved throughout or only in certain phases of the project)*	Head of public services Public services staff member Collections staff member E-resource management staff member Interlibrary loan staff member Technical services staff member Library public relations staff member Outreach services staff member

Resources:

(What is needed to do this work? Consider monetary budget, human resources, training, and technology.)

- Staff time from all project team members
- Excel training for the e-resources management staff member performing data compilation
- COUNTER Release 5 orientation for collections staff performing data analysis

Timeline:

(Who will do what by when?)

August	Current fiscal year's budget becomes available; projections for next fiscal year show likely budget shortfalls
September	Executive sponsor charges project sponsor with

	identifying budget reductions
October	Project sponsor convenes project team and holds project launch meeting, meeting schedule established
November	Project team and project sponsor set project scope, deliverables, and timeline

Project team forms subgroups to focus on data compilation/analysis work and on communications |
| December | Project team identifies desirable data points |
| January–February | Data compilation subgroup members collect institutional data collected (e.g., collection size by subject, data on department sizes/enrollment/degrees awarded)

Communication subgroup, after meeting with various colleagues for input, crafts talking points for library staff to use with external stakeholders |
| January–February | E-resources staff collect available COUNTER usage statistics for databases under review

E-resources staff conduct overlap analysis identifying full-text resources available in other products for databases under review |
| February to early March | E-resources staff compile reports including current and historical usage data, cost data, and fund sources

Communication subgroup develops plan to solicit and assess user feedback |
| March 15 | E-resources staff deliver compiled data for review to data subgroup for initial analysis and evaluation |
| Mid-March to mid-April | All project team members review and analyze data

Subject librarians, public services, and outreach staff get user feedback on resources under review

Head of public services notifies resource providers and/ or consortia whose products are identified as potentially problematic that the resource is under review for potential cancellation |

	E-resources staff review consortial offers available for the products currently under evaluation
Mid-April to May	Communication and data subgroups report back to full project team All project team members discuss user feedback, analyze data, and consider any negotiated offers from vendors and/or consortia Project team drafts various cancellation scenarios and prepares recommendations for the project sponsor and executive sponsor Each scenario includes basics of a communication plan and of the processing/logistical work involved
May	Project team submits report to executive sponsor, including three cancellation scenarios, to executive sponsor
June	Cancellation decisions are made by executive sponsor and reported back to project team Project team submits cancellation decisions to technical services/acquisitions and e-resources staff for processing E-resources staff begin processing cancellations with vendors, consortia, and subscription agents, including updating ILS records and knowledgebase holdings Public services staff and library overall communicate with users, informing them of cancellation outcomes Interlibrary loan staff begin planning to track any potential impacts on borrowing activity by users post-cancellation
July	Cancellations take effect E-resources staff begin confirming post-cancellation access in place for relevant titles and platforms Project team meets to discuss project, identifying pain

	points and successes, and submits final report, including recommendations for future collections review projects, to project sponsor

Project Assessment Plan:

(How will you know whether the project has succeeded or failed? How will this project inform future work?)

- The specific cancellation target of 10% reduction on yearly database spending has been met.
- Technical services and/or e-resources staff have the details necessary to take action on the decisions.
- Project team submits recommendations for conducting future collections reviews.
- Impacts on users as a result of cancellations are being monitored for analysis and any potential response.

APPENDIX B: POTENTIAL DATA POINTS TO CONSIDER

As noted in this chapter, a library's context-specific situation should inform what data is collected and what evaluation processes are put in place. This listing is offered as a non-comprehensive starting place for elements to consider.

Consider how files will be moved within and among staff during a cancellation project as well as be exchanged with vendors, agents, or publishers. Be mindful of which data points various parties will need to take action on decisions. In order to do this work well, some manner of match point or unique identifier should be consistent across all project files. This will allow e-resources management staff to recompile any files or data points that have become disarticulated during the project.

- Resource title
  - ○ Could include individual resource title, a package title, title lists for

included titles

- Unique identifier
  - Often ILS or order number or perhaps a publisher's title number, critical to track titles across different files over the lifespan of a project
- Package or bundle details
  - Are titles ordered in combination or paid on another subscription; is access contingent on other subscriptions?
- Subscription term
- Access model
  - IP-based, limited/unlimited simultaneous users, etc.
- Current cost
  - Difference from list price in the case of negotiated cost
  - Any negotiated annual price caps
- Historical cost
  - If negotiated pricing terms, consider the difference between list price inflation and local/negotiated costs over X years
- Fund source
- Post-cancellation access rights
- Availability in local or third-party archives
- Usage
  - COUNTER reports
  - Non-COUNTER reports
  - Multiple years, to identify trends
- Local indicators of use
  - Could include web page or ILS analytics, proxy logs, discovery layer reports
- Indicators of local publication or research activity
  - Citations by users
  - Citations to users
- Users affiliated with the product (e.g., faculty member on the editorial board)
- Overlap or sources of alternative access

- Coverage in indexing or discovery products
- Open access status
- Impact factor
- Altmetrics
- Subject area
  ◦ Could be from a resource call number, vendor-provided subject headings, or local mapping to meaningful subject areas
- Primary department or user group supported by the resource(s)
- Institutional or community demographics
- User feedback
  ◦ Personal discussions, interviews, user groups, surveys

Nine

Behaviors and Communication Strategies of E-Resources Management Staff

Angela Sidman and Stephanie Willen Brown

We are very different types of librarians who work to make e-resources available to our disparate users. Angela is the director of e-resources and serials management in the Technical Services department at Yale University, serving about 13,000 users, while Stephanie is director of the Park Library, a small departmental library at the University of North Carolina—Chapel Hill that serves about 1,000 students enrolled in UNC's Hussman School of Journalism and Media. The majority of Angela's job responsibilities revolve around the universe of e-resources management, while Stephanie spends only about 10% of her time dealing with e-resources.

Still, we both need many of the skills listed in NASIG's Core Competencies for E-Resources Librarians, starting with knowledge of the lifecycle of e-resources—from acquisitions, budgeting, and accounting, and moving into knowledge of technology, research and assessment, management, trends in licensing and other legal issues related to e-resources, and personal qualities such as "[f]lexibility, open-mindedness and the ability to function in a dynamic, rapidly changing environment" (NASIG, 2013). Our focus for this chapter, however, is the NASIG competency smack in the middle of the list: "effective communication."

NASIG recommends that e-resource librarians should be:

Communicating effectively, promptly, and consistently, verbally and in writing, with a broad range of internal and external audiences: users, colleagues and staff, subscription agents, and vendors; the ERL must be able to tailor the message(s) to the circumstances and to the audience, as needed. (2013)

We agree that soft skills, such as behavioral and communicative skills, are essential to success of the e-resources management staff member, in addition to knowledge of all of the above. In fact, we align these soft skills with those of public services staff, especially when NASIG recommends that the e-resources staff member "tailor the message(s) to the circumstances and to the audience."

Talking to our colleagues in the library and vendor worlds benefits greatly from the following soft skills:

1. All e-resource communication should be **gracious, courteous, and respectful**, to the best of our ability. We like the advice of Harmon regarding email: "Take the time to be nice" (2017). Most of this article will address communication by email, but we recognize that some communication should be done more synchronously, by phone, or even—gasp!—in person. Angela is fond of saying, "it's not just what you do, it's how you do it." Therefore, our advice here applies equally to written and verbal communication.

2. **Relationship and coalition building** with our various stakeholders, from end users to funders, from vendors to subscription agents, including consortium partners and non-library staff elsewhere in our organizations, and—of course—our colleagues in their various roles, from public services to interlibrary loan, financing support, catalogers, and more. The result of this cultivation should lead to the e-resources management staff member being a trusted partner.

3. Who are our **stakeholders and contacts**? As e-resources management staff, we interact with virtually all staff within our libraries, and we also work with a variety of external contacts. Regardless of how much time we spend with e-resources, we both "investigate new con-

tent for purchase," as described in *TERMS*, especially in point number 5, talking to suppliers and vendors (Emery & Stone, 2013).

4. All of our work should be **transparent**. We should communicate clearly with all of our stakeholders, and we should be transparent to all of our internal stakeholders about allocation formulas and budget processes involved, the technology we are using, and the ever-constant change.

5. We should **communicate good news, notifying** our stakeholders that we have finally secured access to The Best Resource Ever. We also must be aware of usage patterns and promote resources that our colleagues or organization know are important but aren't getting sufficient use relative to need and the size of our user base.

6. At the same time, we must also **communicate bad news**, telling our stakeholders what they don't want to hear.

7. **Negotiation and persuasion**. We must shepherd the resource through its entire lifecycle, and that involves getting input from key (and likely diverse) stakeholders, considering other points of view (you say Web of Science, I say Scopus), and considering the organization's values. The process of negotiating the license, of course, involves persuasion and subtle communication skills.

GRACIOUS, COURTEOUS, AND RESPECTFUL COMMUNICATION

We say that communication should be gracious, courteous, and respectful to the best of our ability; what do we mean by that? First, we mean that we should be friendly in our email exchanges. Stephanie often drafts emails by spewing forth exactly what she needs the recipient to know or do; she gets the important elements onto the screen and then takes a breath and inserts a friendly comment about the weekend or the weather to start the email. We don't need to go overboard with the pleasantries, but unless we know the recipient very well, we should include some.

We should also respect the recipient's time and write precisely and with clear questions or action items, so that the recipient knows what is expected in return. As Harmon suggests, we should also "[u]se an intuitive subject line that clearly states the purpose of the message" (2017). In addition, we should know when to reply immediately and when to pause before hitting "send." We should also know when the phone or an in-person visit is more appropriate.

A recent experience highlights this suggestion. Stephanie was asked by her library's serials agent for a status update on payment for the annual invoice. Stephanie emailed her accounting colleague reiterating that the invoice was ready for payment. Moments later, the colleague appeared in Stephanie's office to assure her that the invoice had been submitted for payment; she indicated that she would let Stephanie know when she had more news. Stephanie was grateful for the update but did not immediately reply to the serials agent, preferring to reply to the agent by day's end with an update.

In the above scenario, we see that sometimes an in-person visit is equally effective at conveying information. We also see that it's not always appropriate to reply immediately, although it's important to reply within a reasonable time. In this situation, Stephanie felt that it was more important to reply to the serials agent just once rather than flood her email with multiple replies.

In addition, a courteous email also respects the other person's time. We recommend always including a clear question or action item. Just as Ranganathan's fourth law of library science states that libraries are designed to "[s]ave the time of the reader" (1931), so too should e-resources management staff respect the time of their stakeholders. Courteous and succinct communication respects the recipient's time and doesn't leave them wondering what issue you need resolved.

BUILDING TRUSTED RELATIONSHIPS

Though our roles managing e-resources differ, we both commit time, thought, and energy to building and maintaining strong relationships with our internal and external partners. Stephanie's experience with the serials invoice, where her colleague stopped by to communicate in person, serves as a good example of how having an existing relationship can help you move through a task, gain information, or solve a problem. It means that you are someone people can rely on, trusting you to offer help, advice, or collaboration. In turn, you know that you can count on your partners for the same things. In this section, we will talk about easy things you can do every day that, over time, will help you build trusted relationships around your organization and beyond:

- Arrive prepared for meetings.
- Always give credit where it's due.
- Pump your own gas.
- Practice transparent communication.
- Maintain a policy of "no surprises."

Trust isn't automatic, nor is it a thing that you gain in a single encounter. It is built over time, as colleagues observe your pattern of behavior and actions and you observe theirs. Let's take it as a given that you are following the pattern of respectful communication that Stephanie laid out earlier. Another easy way to show respect for your colleagues and to build their trust is to simply **arrive prepared for meetings**. This can be as easy as sending out an agenda ahead of time if you are the meeting organizer or reading the agenda in advance if you are an attendee. Are there documents you should review before this meeting? Then do so. Questions you might be asked? Take a minute to prepare responses. A small investment in preparation will demonstrate to your supervisor and colleagues that you understand

and are responding to shared priorities and take your role in the organization seriously.

Another easy way to build trust is to **give credit where it's due**. In
working with e-resources, very little is done in isolation. People may not
always remember if you thanked them, but they will absolutely remember if they feel you represented their work as your own. If someone in IT
helps you with a difficult EZproxy stanza, credit them when you report
how the access problem was solved. If a staff person has a great idea about
a new way to do work, acknowledge their contribution if you implement
the change.

Shapiro says, "This concept of appreciation is incredibly powerful
in predicting everything from marital stability over time to organizational success, to team work, effective productive teamwork over time"
(n.d.). We agree—and although it takes a little extra effort to share the
credit for successes, it does let your partners know you acknowledge
and appreciate their work, and others will (rightly!) see you as a good
collaborator.

Angela once worked for an organization where there was an in-office
shorthand for people who were good collaborators: They were said to
"**pump their own gas**." These were the people who did their home-
work and constructively attempted to solve problems on their own before
asking for assistance. Not coincidentally, these were the people whom
everyone was always ready to help, as they had earned the reputation
as trusted partners. The opposite of this, of course, were those library
staff who did not pump their own gas. This group was prone to finding
problems (and fault) without wanting to then put in the time or effort
to find a solution. The logic of pumping your own gas is the same as
that of arriving prepared for meetings. An investment of time and a bit
of problem-solving effort will demonstrate to your colleagues that you
respect their time and aren't just trying to shift the burden of difficult
problems but are, in fact, trying to find a constructive solution.

OUR STAKEHOLDERS

As e-resources management staff, we have **multiple stakeholders**. All stakeholders have different reasons to relate with us, and our communication must differ to match their needs.

Stakeholders include our colleagues within the library. Subject librarians and frontline service staff are often the ones who want a new resource or who notify us of a problem with access to a resource. They may be acting on their own, or they may be relaying a message from an end user such as a faculty member, student, or community member. Colleagues in technical services must catalog the services that we license, while colleagues in information technology may be responsible for adding (or removing) a resource from the library's website or database locator. We may need to communicate with interlibrary loan staff to assess the impact of a resource on that service. We may need to share a license with our legal team before access is completed. We need to review the cost details with our financial colleagues, for issues ranging from making the final decision on a purchase or to ensuring that payment is made.

There can be multiple external stakeholders as well. Primary among these are our vendors or subscription agents. They want to do business with us because they want to make a sale, which is often essential to their work. Their jobs also may be to resolve problems that arise; even if these stakeholders aren't primarily responsible for selling to us, they are highly focused on customer satisfaction.

We may be partners in one or more consortia, and if any of a consortium's mission is resource sharing, then our work is tied to that of our consortial partners. We might be part of a buying group such as NERL, NC LIVE, or LYRASIS. In some cases, the consortium staff will do the licensing and negotiation, and we in e-resources management function as the liaison between the consortium and our internal stakeholders. In other cases, we may do some e-resources management tasks on behalf of our consortium. Regardless, consortium staff can be our stakeholders and associates; it's possible that the consortium's members may also be some of our stakeholders.

Non-library employees elsewhere in our organization may also be our stakeholders. These could include accounting staff responsible for our budget or legal counsel providing licensing support. These could also be administrators above us in the power chain such as deans, provosts, town or county managers, department heads, or vice presidents. These stakeholders could have financial interests in our work or might want a particular resource for their work. We might be sharing the cost of a resource with a non-library entity, such as a faculty member on a grant.

It is important to consider the wide variety of stakeholders, because we may need to communicate differently with different groups. We would communicate information about OpenURL availability differently with catalogers than we would when responding to an outage reported by a faculty member; we might discuss licensing restrictions differently with legal counsel than we would with a reference liaison. This harkens back to our reference skills, where we must adapt our message to the recipient. If we have a long-standing relationship with a vendor, we will adopt a casual tone when emailing about a problem; likewise, if we are writing a new consortium colleague, we should communicate with more clarity—and perhaps use the telephone rather than email to initiate a complicated interaction.

TRANSPARENCY

E-resources management staff often work in areas that can seem mysterious to those in other parts of the organization, with responsibilities for technology, budgets, and changing workflows. By practicing clear and **transparent communication** on these and other complex topics, we build trust in how you share information, make decisions, and allocate services. Let's take the example of budgets. Angela worked for a consortium where the formula for dividing costs for shared e-resources was based on weighted calculations of measurable factors, including FTE, collection budget, and usage of two specific journal packages (a stand-in for research intensity). Every year the formula was reviewed, updated, and approved, so that when the time came for group purchasing, all participants understood exactly how the cost of their share had been reached. Versions of the allocation formula were in place long before Angela arrived, and its use continued after her departure. Though not all consortium managers were equally enthusiastic about every purchase or their comparative pricing allocations, the process was seen as fair, and buying as a consortium was understood to be beneficial by all. This is a testament to how a clear, transparent, collaborative approach to a sensitive subject can build trust in the process (group purchases), its agents (collection development, acquisitions, and e-resources management staff), and its results (a substantial shared collection).

When Angela meets with new staff, one of the first things she tells them about is the rule of "**no surprises**." She operates under the assumption that her supervisor would prefer to hear about problems, mistakes, or unexpected circumstances of any kind directly from her rather than hearing it for the first time from an outside source. Her staff are expected to operate under the same principle. If you want people to trust you, and to trust your judgment, you need to be good about flagging information that others may need and passing it along in a timely manner. No one wants to feel ambushed, as Angela sometimes was by a coworker who had a habit of using stakeholder meetings to announce that she had discovered technical problems in other people's work. Because she had not shared this information prior to the meeting, the problem diagnosis was not even always accurate and perceived problems could have been talked through quickly, one on one. Because these announcements happened in public settings, though, the misinformation was difficult to undo and the feelings of distrust around this colleague ran deep.

PROMOTION

Some library staff consider "promotion" to be unnecessary, believing instead that users will magically find what they need from the library's website or from a library staff member. Stephanie works with public relations faculty and students and believes that promotion is essential. One example demonstrates the need for promotion in libraries. Stephanie was teaching a class of university juniors and seniors and as part of her presentation, she pointed out the extensive streaming media resources available at the university. At the end of the class, one student piped up and said, "I had no idea we had all these streaming videos—and I'm a senior documentary major."

This kind of feedback is heartbreaking, because the library has spent vast sums of money purchasing, licensing, and making these resources available on the website. And yet, the primary audience is completely unaware of the existence of these streaming documentaries. Some staff might argue that it is the students' or faculty members' responsibility to become aware of the resources.

Instead, we believe that we library staff must make sure that our users are aware of the resources that we offer. Just as with communication with various stakeholders, we must tailor our messages to different audiences. In this case, Stephanie immediately created promotional flyers for the university's streaming media, targeted to students and faculty in the documentary filmmaking program. She posted the print flyers—with small tear-offs for students to take—on the walls and prepared social media posts highlighting these resources for all students.

Promotion is essential to informing our users of our resources. The adage from the film *Field of Dreams*, "if we build it [or buy it], they will come," no longer applies. Instead, we must see to it that our resources are promoted. Angela isn't directly responsible for promoting resources that she licenses at Yale, but Stephanie works with her communication team to promote resources to her users. For more on promotion of library resources, refer to Mathews' excellent book, *Marketing Today's Academic Library.* If you do marketing like Stephanie does, you'll find it useful; if you don't promote your resources, like Angela, you might suggest this to your colleagues that do.

TELLING PEOPLE WHAT THEY DON'T WANT TO HEAR

As library workers, we like to say "YES!" to everything. We like to offer resources that our users want, and we work hard to make that happen. However, there are times when we must say no, either because the licensing terms don't work out, or because the cost of the resource is too high, or for other reasons. We offer some examples here of when we've had to say no to a database that our users wanted, as well as some of the ways we've communicated that to our users.

There is a print resource essential to all students at UNC's Hussman School of Journalism & Media; students are required to purchase this book and use it for many classes. The book itself is reissued annually with some changes. The library purchases three copies of the book every year, in an effort to make it easy for students to consult the library's copy. This source has an online component, but it's been nearly impossible to license access. Stephanie communicated with the vendor, explaining that the terms were not acceptable and suggesting alternate language. The vendor was similarly unable to accept Stephanie's suggested language. So, Stephanie replied with the following note:

> "Thanks for the information. As I mentioned over the phone, I cannot accept those terms. I know the Library's print [resource] will get a lot of use!

"Thanks to you and C. for your help." (S.W. Brown, personal communication, 2019)

That interaction was challenging, and eleven years later continues to be challenging for Stephanie to explain this decision to users. Stephanie concisely and politely says that she and the vendor could not come to terms on licensing, therefore she suggests users access the print resource instead.

COMMUNICATING BAD NEWS

E-resources save shelf space, are available anywhere at any time, and can be searched and used in ways that strongly support teaching, learning, and research. They also go up in price, are subject to mergers and acquisitions, may have terrible user interfaces, and sometimes just plain break. In other words, there are many occasions large and small when e-resources staff might be the bearer of unwelcome tidings. That said, there are better and worse ways to communicate bad news. By **staying calm and presenting the facts**, an e-resources management staff member models professionalism, demonstrates expertise, and earns confidence.

When access goes down on an e-resource platform or in a linking or discovery system, Angela always appreciates when the vendor makes a quick acknowledgement that there is a known problem, describes the problem's scope (All customers? All products?), and estimates what the timeline might be for resolving the issue. This is the same information that she tries to include in her own internal messaging about access issues. When access problems occur, they are generally out of the e-resources management team's direct control. In those situations, the best service we can give our users and stakeholders is to alert them that there is a known issue, provide alternate means of access if any exist, and give a potential timeline for access returning to normal. Depending on the size of the institution and the scope of the service interruption, it can help to have predetermined contacts based on the scale of a problem. Perhaps a specific subject librarian for a niche product, all public services staff for a heavily used resource, and staff-wide or clear external announcements for a prolonged outage with serious user impact. Once the problem has been resolved, following up with an all-clear message is the final piece in a well-organized communication plan (see Appendix A for example elements of a communications plan).

Talking about platform outages is relatively easy, because they are often out of our control. It is much harder to communicate about problems of our own making. Sometimes a resource is unavailable because the invoice got stuck and we haven't yet paid the bill. If that is the case, the best general policy is to treat this as you would an external problem: Give the facts, provide a timeline for resolving the problem, and offer alternative access if any exists. The worst news that Angela has had to deliver involved money. An institution she worked for was in negotiation to make a substantial e-book purchase directly with the publisher. Licensing carried on for several months. So many, in fact, that the deal did not make it over the finish line in time for that fiscal year, and the deal was declared dead. Even worse, the money that had been earmarked for this purchase was absorbed back into the larger budget, meaning a purchase in the following year was far from certain. Angela had to explain this both internally, to people who wanted this content, and externally, to the publisher's representatives who, after months of work, had unexpectedly lost a major sale. Though she dreaded it, Angela called her sales representative and personally explained that the deal had fallen through and that the funding that had been in place this year was gone and might not be available again. This helped keep the trusted relationship between partners secure, even in the face of bad news. In the next fiscal year, the university and publisher returned to the negotiation table and did successfully complete a major purchase.

NEGOTIATION AND PERSUASION

Negotiation is a skill that most e-resources management staff think of in terms of license agreements and business terms. There are lightweight and practical ways to employ negotiation in your daily work, as well. If you know what you want, where you are flexible, and what your absolute drop-dead issues are, then you are ready to negotiate! Library staff want to say yes when faced with a request, but it's not always a practical response. This is particularly true when saying yes creates an ongoing commitment of your time or resources. When faced with a big ask, Angela often runs through a mental checklist:

- Do I have something (time, resources, expertise) to contribute?
- Does this further any of my goals (for myself or my department)?
- Does this further a broader institutional goal?

If saying yes is easy, say yes! If it isn't a clear yes, though, negotiation skills can help. For example, if asked to participate in a time-consuming project, a library staff member might think:

- I could contribute expertise but am worried about this taking me away from other work.
- This presents an opportunity to work with new people and learn more about an area that interests me.
- My institution has clearly prioritized this project.

The conversation that follows could then be shaped by this thinking. "I know this is a crucial project, and I want to participate but am worried about getting everything done. Can we talk about how I might balance this with my existing work?" This opens the door to a conversation about how you might re-prioritize your work or hand off pieces during the project period. If you know what you want to do and are prepared to do a bit of trading, you can often arrive at a solution that ultimately helps everyone.

The final soft skill we want to cover is **persuasion**. For our purposes, think of persuasion as the art and science of bringing people along with you on a journey to a destination you all wish to reach. There are a lot of ways to introduce change in a workplace. Some methods, like laying down edicts, can result in immediate changes and may grant you short term success, but these tactics aren't likely to yield good long-term results. By contrast, persuasion may require a higher investment of time at the outset but can lead to much brighter long-term prospects, as everyone has agreed on what the outcome should be.

The key to persuasion isn't talking, but listening. Do you need to get people to buy in to a big new package deal? Do you want people to successfully migrate to a new tool or adopt a new policy? Once a need has taken shape and you have a sense of what needs to be done, take it on the road. Identify key stakeholders (even give a little honest flattery and mention that they are key stakeholders!), explain the work you are contemplating, and then ask for their comments. Even better, circulate a draft document to your stakeholders in advance of these conversations, so that they arrive prepared and ready to give thoughtful feedback. Then, listen to what they have to say, ask questions to help tease out any missing pieces, and do your best to incorporate what you learned into your next round of planning. Depending on what you are doing, you can circulate a second draft or work plan so that your stakeholders can see that you took their feedback seriously. When you present your new policy or project for more formal approval, many of the people in the room will already know the background and will be in support of your plans. For a major project, particularly one that impacts systems or public services, you can continue to iterate on this theme, receiving feedback from increasingly wide circles as you progress to implementation.

CONCLUSION

In this chapter, we have described many ways in which you, the e-resources management staff member, can communicate effectively and become a trusted partner within your organization. By communicating courteously, respecting colleagues' time, and reacting calmly and competently to whatever the day throws at you, you can establish yourself as a colleague whose knowledge and professionalism garner respect. Building on this same skill set, you can go even further and use negotiation and persuasion techniques to solve problems and achieve specific goals. The keys to this are listening, incorporating feedback, and having a clear sense of your personal and institutional priorities.

Soft skills are NOT about soft-pedaling, glad-handing, or insincerity. Rather, they are about collegial tone, transparent communication, and trusted relationships. In this chapter, we laid out how this suite of communication skills and a good dose of organizational awareness can help us be better in our jobs. These skills augment our knowledge and experience, allowing us to do more, solve bigger problems, and get better results.

CITATIONS AND FURTHER READING

Emery, J., & Stone, G. (2013). *Techniques for electronic resource management.* Chicago: ALA TechSource. https://doi.org/10.5860/ltr.49n2

Fisher, P. H., Pride, M. M., & Miller, E. G. (2005). *Blueprint for your library marketing plan: A guide to help you survive and thrive.* American Library Association.

This book covers many elements of a library marketing plan, and while it is largely designed to market the library to library users (academic and public), elements of the book are useful for promoting e-resources internally and externally. They have developed a comprehensive library marketing plan from work by the "father of marketing" Philip Kotler.

Harmon, S. (2017). How to make sure your emails give the right impression. *Harvard Business Review.* https://hbr.org/2017/02/how-to-make-sure-your-emails-give-the -right-impression

Harmon provides four common-sense tips for writing effective emails, such as writing clear subject lines and topic sentences; clarifying any actions you'd like the recipient to take; and taking the time to be nice.

Ibach, M. (2020). *An introduction to creating a library marketing plan* [Video]. Wisconsin Valley Library Service. https://www.youtube.com/watch?v=9q_fbeHxaTI

Reassuring and helpful introduction to library marketing plans, based on Kathy Dempsy's "Cycle of True Marketing."

Mathews, B. (2009). *Marketing today's academic library: A bold new approach to communicating with students.* Chicago: American Library Association.

Mathews researched effective marketing strategies from disciplines outside the library profession. His approach focuses on students rather than libraries and is written in an engaging style. Mathews doesn't focus specifically on promoting e-resources to students, but the book offers several great ideas for general marketing.

NASIG. (2013). *NASIG core competencies for electronic resources librarians.*https://www .nasig.org/Competencies-Eresources

Posner, M. (2015). Emailing someone you don't know. http://miriamposner.com /dh101f15/index.php/tutorials-and-resources/emailing-someone-you-I-know/

Helpful advice addressed to undergraduate students in a UCLA class. Includes how to address recipients you don't know (formal); length of first email (short); and offering options for how to reply (email or phone). Not directly related to library staff or e-resource work but useful, nonetheless.

Ranganathan, S. R. (1931). *The five laws of library science.* Madras Library Association. http://hdl.handle.net/2027/uc1.$b99721

Shapiro, D. (n.d.). The five core concerns of negotiation [Video]. https://bigthink.com /videos/the-five-core-concerns-of-negotiation

Shapiro is a Harvard psychologist and founder/director of the Harvard International Negotiation Program. He briefly describes his five core concerns of negotiation. Watch a short video or read the transcript, as he describes the value of appreciation, autonomy, affiliation, status, and role in negotiations.

APPENDIX A: ELEMENTS OF A COMMUNICATION PLAN

A Google search yields many examples and templates for a communication plan. However, all plans should include the following:

- **Context**. What is the current situation in terms of communications and what you need to communicate? For example: What is the problem you're trying to solve, and what is the solution?
- **Goal.** What is the objective you're trying to achieve with this communication?
- **Audience.** Who are the key people this communication is for?
- **Distribution status.** What is the communication's distribution status, and how will you note this? For example, is it internal to a specific group or organization, is it confidential or public?
- **Communication channels and mechanics**. What are the information types and distribution methods available, and which ones are effective for your audience and your message? For example: electronic discussion group, email, website, press release, social media, etc.
- **Timeline and frequency.** Considering your audience and the urgency of your messaging, by when should each task be completed, and when should it recur (if at all)?
- **Responsibilities.** Who is responsible for each task pertaining to the communication?
- **Retention.** Where will the final copy of the communication reside for future reference and quick access if appropriate?

Ten

Trends, Challenges, and Opportunities in E-Resources Management

Jenifer S. Holman

Keeping up with new trends in library work and e-resources management isn't just a stretch goal for e-resources practitioners, it's a skill codified in the NASIG Core Competencies for E-Resources Librarians (2013). While no one staff member (or even one department) should be expected to embody all the competencies in this ambitious document, change is a constant companion for those who work with e-resources. Keeping pace, therefore, is a valuable and necessary asset. In addition to keeping up with trends, a large array of challenges and opportunities crowd today's e-resources landscape.

Those who work with e-resources, perhaps more so than other library staff, have weathered years of steady change while evolving from work that was historically located in technical services, managing serials, or growing out of the public services side as experts in database searching. Many library staff doing the work of e-resources management may have widely varying titles that don't indicate "electronic resources" at all. While e-resources workers continue to be sorted into technical services departments on many organizational charts, position responsibilities frequently overlap with both public services and collection development. In spanning these three areas, e-resources staff have unique opportunities to bridge the divides that may still exist amongst these areas and make important contributions in each (Verminski & Blanchat, 2017). Specific challenges and opportunities that e-resources workers might encounter include staffing challenges, co-operative opportunities, collections as services, transformative agreements, and project management. The future may look very different from the one envisioned here, but actively engaging with coworkers to share ideas and possibilities while embracing shared beliefs and values (encompassed in the library's mission) positions an e-resources team to thrive in a host of possible futures.

STAFFING/ORGANIZATIONAL STRUCTURE

In some smaller libraries, e-resources management may remain a single position in a larger technical services department. Having one worker responsible for the lifecycle of the majority of purchases and licensed resources may pose workload challenges, especially if there still exists a much larger group of library staff who continue to manage a decreasing number of print resources. With some library budgets reflecting 75% of new resources being acquired electronically as far back as 2013 (Gremmels, 2013), managers can articulate a strong value proposition for adding staff lines to manage the lifecycle of e-resources. All libraries face budget constraints, and whether the outlook is staffing reductions or even mergers with IT departments, it is critical for e-resources workers to continually demonstrate value to their institutions, and for library administrations to appropriately staff the management of electronic collections. E-resources staff might take two tracks in facing this challenge:

- working together with technical services coworkers to reallocate workflow responsibilities while more forcefully demonstrating the value of the work; and/or
- sharing and distributing the work between multiple institutions through cooperative agreements (e.g., memoranda of understanding or consortia).

DEMONSTRATING AND MAPPING VALUE

E-resources workers can use their strong communication skills and a solid understanding of position responsibilities to craft a compelling message to their managers and library directors that calls for moving or keeping organizational resources in the technical services area (whether that is still within a library or even in the IT department). While it has always been important for library staff to articulate institutional value, today's information environment heightens the sense that institutions must demonstrate return on investment to survive (Murray, 2017). E-resources staff should have an elevator pitch ready to share with their manager, administrators, boards, faculty, and their peers that clearly communicates not only what e-resources works involves, but especially *why* it's important. As an example of what this value statement might look like in a college library, when preparing for a departmental visit from our provost, each technical services staff member at my library pulled together a five-minute elevator pitch to briefly communicate what they did. In preparing for this visit, I reread a wonderful post by Salo (2011) on the value of library praxis. We ended up pulling a particularly empowering quote from Salo's piece and using it as a departmental motto of sorts, now prominently displayed on our office bulletin board: "Because of what [we] do, more people can find and use more information. The work [we] do changes the way the world works and learns, every single day."

A tangible way to show value as well as build a strong team is to start an ongoing culture of continuous education. (One of my favorite resources for the how and why of team building is Lencioni's *The Five Dysfunctions of a Team*, published in 2002.) Conducting an e-resources management skills inventory in your unit is a great place to begin team building. As Sutton and Sullenger discuss, using the NASIG core competencies to map the skills of their work unit enabled staff members to quickly visualize skills gaps and silos (2017). Depending on the available staffing in any given unit, the results of such a skills inventory provides a compelling case to either add FTE to help cover tasks or to lobby for existing staff to get specific training so they can take on additional tasks, reskill the library's existing staff, and/or enter collaborative staffing agreements. Conducting the inventory as a unit also celebrates the unique contributions of each team member while providing clear guidance on areas that team members need more training in. For special library staff, the NASIG competencies may not go far enough. The Special Libraries Association (SLA) offers a certificate course in competitive and decision intelligence and has been at the forefront of supporting corporate library staff in demonstrating value to their employers.

E-resources managers can also build value by emphasizing their impact on users. Through troubleshooting forms, short integrated videos in database descriptions, and descriptive notes on e-journal records, e-resources staff regularly not only interact with users but provide quality, concise instruction at the point of need. Through troubleshooting form responses, staff members not only guide users to needed content, but also provide teaching moments on everything from navigating to appropriate databases to explaining how articles are published (e.g., preprints vs. post-prints). Providing our users with point-of-need services is one of the most powerful tools e-resources staff possess. Creating short videos showing how to locate book reviews in a certain database or how to quickly navigate a complex interface to create a list of businesses by geographical area saves users valuable time. Staff in special libraries can take leadership roles in making sure their organizations have training and access to the latest tools and resources on decision intelligence. E-resources staff continue to play an important role in providing user services within their organizations.

LOOKING BEYOND YOUR ORGANIZATION

With so many similar organizations offering the same e-resources through the same cloud-based management systems, many opportunities exist to partner with other institutions and share expertise and job responsibilities via memoranda of understanding or other agreements. Libraries—and public libraries in particular—have already been sharing e-resources management responsibilities through group licensing. Whether it's through Lyrasis, Minitex, MCLS, or another statewide or national consortium, these entities have been helping smaller libraries get better deals with vendors for many years. Many states have consortia that license and manage large groups of e-books and databases available to all users in that state. Those consortia not only provide a valuable service to all state residents but can also use their power to help libraries get discounts on additional content from those same vendors.

Cooperative licensing is just the beginning for cooperative projects, however. Public libraries, for example, have been pioneers in the purchase, licensing, and delivery of e-books for large consortia consisting of all kinds of libraries, including academic and school libraries. An example of such cross-library cooperation is the Marmot Library Network's adoption of Jamie LaRue's "Douglas County Model" that sought to alleviate the usability issues from multiple e-book interfaces by creating a local e-book server that would host all centrally purchased e-books (Thomas & Noble, 2016). While ultimately not successful, the experiences of the Marmot Library Network provide a thoughtful example of the power of cooperation.

A more recent project that has had early success is LEAP's SimplyE, which is making great progress toward its goal orancoevanc[ing] a national digital platform to help library patrons find, borrow, and consume the largest variety and inventory of content possible" (English & Richardson, 2017). A founding partner in LEAP (the Library E-content Access Project), the New York Public Library (NYPL) is using SimplyE as the user interface for all of its e-books (Neuer, 2016). Several public library systems have signed on to SimplyE as partners with the NYPL, and Amigos Library Services (https://www.amigos.org/simplye) is offering technical support as well as the necessary infrastructure to any public library interested in implementing this platform.

With libraries already sharing their e-resources, why not share their staff? Public libraries lead the way here, and if you find yourself working on e-resources for a public library, your position may be housed within a consortium providing services to many different libraries.

Through formal agreements, organizations of all types may share e-resources staff to manage day-to-day tasks. Our cloud-based resource management systems can be accessed and managed remotely. While this sort of cooperative e-resources management appears to be a current reality reserved mostly for large consortia, there is little reason why a group of like-minded libraries could not come together and pool their human resources for increased efficiencies and better experiences for library users and for the greater good of all. This efficiency is so compelling that sharing management of e-resources could be an important consideration when migrating to a new library management system. For example, by using the "Network Zone" functionality in Ex Libris's Alma, a staff member at one location can manage the resources for the entire consortium. As an example of how sharing a Network Zone saves time, one staff member working at the network level can activate and manage the databases that all consortium members share, saving much duplicated effort.

Reporting and statistics gathering is another area that would benefit from increased collaboration. As many libraries may gather the same statistics for reporting to ACRL, their library boards, or their provosts each year, library staff could also share standard queries for gathering these data on systems like Alma, which allows for analytics reports to be shared and customized locally. E-resources management staff will have ample opportunities to leverage their expertise in the future, providing value not only to their home institutions, but perhaps far beyond their own walls. The ultimate collaborative opportunity for libraries may be the FOLIO (Future of Libraries is Open) project, in which member libraries, vendors, consortia, and developers are working together to build an open-source uniform resource management system from the ground up (FOLIO, 2018). In just a few years, FOLIO has added an impressive list of partner libraries (https://www.folio.org/community/support/) and continues to grow, both in numbers of library adoptions and in functionality. FOLIO is not only a great example of how powerful libraries can be when they join forces, but also provides a shining example of the tangible outcomes that follows when libraries lead with their values.

COOPERATIVE PURCHASING/COLLECTIONS AS A SERVICE

While various library leaders continue to prognosticate about the future, there is little doubt that the very nature of libraries is changing. With decreasing or static library budgets being the rule rather than the exception, staff in all types of libraries need to build a responsive collection that serves the institution's mission—whether that is focused on teaching and student success, or research, or both. What will e-resources management look like in this new landscape that Lorcan Dempsey (2016) has termed the inside-out library and the facilitated collection? The skill sets of e-resources workers, with one foot in technical services and another in public services, can serve as an important bridge from a library with an owned collection to a library with a facilitated collection (Dempsey, 2016, p. 353). The many different data sets, databases, e-book packages, and streaming video platforms licensed by e-resources staff comprise the base of the new facilitated collection. Those tools that e-resources workers use to make these resources available to their users, whether it's an A-Z database list, an EZproxy bookmarklet, a LibGuide explaining how to use Zotero, streaming video services, or their very presence on a research team, are all ways to leverage these collections as services.

The inside-out library, with its focus on the facilitated collection, will make room for a larger mix of open collections. This shift from ownership to access creates room for e-resources workers to reflect on their values and consider walking away from large "Big Deal" packages. E-resources workers have opportunities to change course in how they currently build their collections and lead with their values. Libraries could optimize budgets to fund open access initiatives before licensing for-profit packages. This shift in budget priorities would clearly communicate library values. While budgets are always stretched thin, e-resources workers can play an important role by placing priorities on open access publishing endeavors such as Lever Press (https://www.leverpress.org/) or SCOAP[3] (https://scoap3.org/). Supporting open access initiatives before supporting large commercial publishers, as the MIT Libraries have done (Finnie, 2016), reflects library values and lays important groundwork in moving to a facilitated collection.

Virginia's Academic Library Consortium (VIVA) has a contract framework in place in which they ask publishers to reduce journal package pricing by the percentage of content that is available open access and authored by VIVA members. As they have said, "[w]hy should VIVA or its members pay for content for which cost has previously been paid or publisher costs have already been otherwise recovered to make the article openly available?" (O'Gara et al, 2019). UnSub, a tool created by Heather Piwowar and Jason Priem, aims to empower library workers to cancel Big Deal packages altogether. Unsub is a "data dashboard that helps libraries forecast, explore, and optimize their alternatives to the Big Deal, so they can unsubscribe with confidence" (Etshmaier et al., 2020, p. 341). Of concern for e-resources workers and their teams is the increase in work that will follow Big Deal cancellations. As Maranville and Diaz argue, "...workflows after a Big Deal are altered, increased, and particularly difficult to absorb for short-staffed units" (2021, p. 209). New models may save collection dollars, and prioritize library values, but e-resources staff should expect and plan for an increased workload.

E-BOOKS AS A SERVICE

We are a long way from the advent of the Gutenberg Project and those first e-books that were unformatted and unappealing plain text. The open

educational resources (OER) movement has helped e-books gain acceptance through the simple message that students can no longer afford to
continue purchasing traditional printed textbooks. Additionally, library
staff can continue to advocate for students as textbook publishers attempt
to control access to electronic textbooks and bypass the used textbook
market through an emerging model known as inclusive access (SPARC,
2021; Swaak, 2021). While many library users continue to prefer printed
books, e-books have shown their worth as a convenience when lugging
heavy print books around proves a chore, and have been a necessity
during pandemic lockdowns. E-resources staff can provide an important
service by making e-books easier to use.

If we have learned anything about e-books, it's that simply accepting
publisher interfaces at face value is not a winning strategy. E-resource
staff must be willing to step up their marketing and education efforts
to make available tools that will enable our users to fully embrace the
benefits of e-books. In addition to working with our vendors to create
better user interfaces, library staff can highlight available tools to optimize use of academic e-books. Hypothes.is (https://web.hypothes.is/) is
a particularly important tool for taking notes and annotating text. It's in-
triguing because it opens the door for students to not only annotate texts,
but to share their notes and highlighted passages as a community, asking each other questions and learning from each other. Along with OER
initiatives, such tools provide the foundation for some exciting new de-
velopments in the areas of teaching and learning. By integrating links to
Hypothes.is and user guides for e-books into our database lists and bibli-
ographic data, library workers can provide needed services for our users
at their point of need.

As libraries explore collections as a service, e-resources staff have an
important role to play in making sure information is available to users
in the format and at the time that they need it. One way to think of
collections as a service is to focus on the public services aspects of managing e-resources. In addition to the value-added instructional services that

e-resources management staff embed in resource descriptions or through user interactions, they also play an important role in marketing resources to other library staff. Specifically, to successfully roll out a new electronic collection, the e-resources management staffer must sell it to the staff. Mortimore and Skinner argue that "… how technical services handles rollouts directly impacts colleagues' and patrons' understanding and awareness of resources as well as their expectations for technical services' role in mediating and supporting them" (2017, p. 166). Through adept marketing of library resources, e-resources staff can connect to their users in new ways, learning valuable information about their users while offering a distinctly valuable service to this user community (Kennedy & LaGuardia, 2018). The rapid ramp-up of streaming video services during the COVID-19 pandemic provides a timely example of a new service rollout in support of a facilitated, inside-out library.

Lastly, this shift to collections as service opens the door for library workers to partner with faculty and other stakeholders in the creation and dissemination of scholarship. E-resources management staff members often have long relationships with a variety of publishers, both open access and for-profit, and through the licensing process most explicitly, they can lobby for and respond to the needs of their researchers. Moving forward, e-resources management staff need to possess a thorough understanding of changes in scholarly communication, the rise of the OER movement, and faculty/stakeholder needs for assistance and education about their roles in the publication process. As Goben (2017) says, "…where I spend my highest energies and my emphases impacts the future work that I will have the opportunity to do with my patrons and at my institution. My default is *with*. Let's work together."

TRANSFORMATIVE AGREEMENTS

Library budgets continue to be slowly and steadily consumed by the cost of journal subscriptions, especially large journal packages. Although one might expect journal costs to start decreasing as more researchers pay to publish their work open access, that has not yet happened. Instead, many publishers continue to profit from traditional library subscriptions, while adding an additional revenue stream from article processing fees (through gold OA). Nearly twenty years after Frazier (2001) coined the term " Big Deal" to refer to large, expensive journal subscription packages, European libraries and consortia (e.g., https://oa2020.org/ and https://www.coalition-s.org/) have led the call to end this "double-dipping" by flipping scholarly publication from a subscription-based model to an open access model. In this new, open access model, researchers and/or their institutions pay publication costs while readers read for free. While these ideas may have germinated in Europe's centrally funded higher education environment, colleges and universities in the United States are increasingly signing on to these "transformative" agreements.

In these new license agreements, libraries or library consortia agree to split their subscription costs into two different accounts. One account pays for the traditional subscription costs, while the other account funds researchers' article processing charges (APCs). The APC account can then be managed either at one library or at the consortium level. How the money is distributed varies, and these deals could easily result in a library paying more money to publishers in the short term. O'Gara and Osterman (2019) caution that leaving publisher monopolies in place while removing the market power of consortia could push any cost savings well into the future. For small institutions, it remains unproven if local publishing activity would be high enough to make this model attractive (Machovec, 2019). If the APC account were funded with annual percentage increases, as an example, the incentive to smaller institutions could be that the publisher would most likely keep the increases as low as possible once that money goes into the APC account. Another compelling argument might be thinking that helping to fund an APC account contributes to the greater good and aligns with library values. However, Farley et al (2021) takes such wishful thinking to task when they bust several myths about transformative agreements and urge extreme caution before participating in them. Read and publish agreements are still new, yet they are a development to which e-resources management staff will want to give close attention.

CHANGE MANAGEMENT/PROJECT MANAGEMENT

As information professionals who not only survive but seemingly thrive during times of change, many e-resources management staff have an affinity for being organizational change managers and project managers. Effective e-resources managers possess the organizational, leadership, and process thinking to become leaders in their libraries during transitions to new library systems or even rise to leadership positions within the library. Whether it's scrum, agile, or more traditional Gantt chart–like project management, e-resources management staff are well suited to lead such projects with grace and enthusiasm. While well-suited for the role of project manager, e-resources managers may not have any formal training in this area and many not even think of their work as project management. Project management, however, can provide valuable resources and techniques to add to a management toolkit. Good communication is essential for the success of any project and "[p]roject management provides a common language that everyone can understand" (Maddox Abbott & Laskowski, 2014, p. 175). Whether you are anticipating a project or already have one scheduled, it's critical to get training on how to learn the language of project management to avoid feeling overextended and disorganized (Vinopal, 2012). For a succinct look at how librarianship and project management intersect, Schacter (2004) offers an excellent introduction. Daugherty and Hines (2018) offer a more expansive view of the connections between project management and libraries. Their contributors offer definitions of project management principles as they apply to libraries as well as a variety of case studies. E-resources managers should take advantage of opportunities to receive training in project management as well. The Electronic Resources & Libraries conference sometimes has workshops on project management. LinkedIn Learning (https://www.linkedin.com/learning/) is also a great choice.

ABOVE ALL ... STAY CURRENT AND NEVER STOP LEARNING

As the library landscape continues to shift under our feet, how do e-resources staff members stay current? In addition to the usual advice to monitor relevant online discussion lists and stay current with the published literature, don't overlook Twitter.

Twitter, for all its faults, serves as an excellent way to check in on conferences that you aren't able to attend, to keep up with happenings in the library landscape, and even to track vendor offerings and system outages. In addition to these, developing a short list of favorite library-focused voices is another way to stay in the loop. Following are a few representative examples:

- Electronic Resources & Libraries Conference: @ERandL
- Charleston Conference: @chsconf
- Lorcan Dempsey: @lorcanD
- Stephen Francoeur: @s_francoeur
- Dorothea Salo: @LibSkrat
- Jessamyn West: @jessamyn

Most importantly, e-resources management staff can stay current by taking advantage of continuing education opportunities. As mentioned above, LinkedIn Learning offers many courses in various software packages, programming languages, and even project management. Some other opportunities are listed below.

- Electronic Resources & Libraries (https://www.electroniclibrarian.org /conference-info/) has both pre- and post-conference workshops.
- Library Juice Academy offers a variety of affordable online courses (http://libraryjuiceacademy.com/courses.php).
- Sarah Durrant offers a highly regarded course on negotiation (http:// www.sarahdurrant.co.uk/negotiation-skills-for-librarians-online/).

The American Library Association's Core Division offers low-cost professional development webinars (http://www.ala.org/core/ce /webinars). As of 2021, the predecessor of Core, the Association for Library Collections and Technical Services (ALCTS), still offered free access to its webinar recordings (http://www.ala.org/alcts /confevents/past/webinar).

These recordings offer an excellent overview of topics including licensing, management, programming languages, and open access. No matter what realities the future holds for libraries, e-resources management staff appear poised to take advantage of opportunities and rise above the many challenges facing our libraries today.

CITATIONS AND FURTHER READING

Daugherty, A., & Hines, S. (2018). *Project management in the library workplace.* Emerald Publishing.

Dempsey, L. (2016). Library collections in the life of the user: Two directions. *LIBER Quarterly, 26*(4), 338–359. https://doi.org/10.18352/lq.10170

English, J., & Richardson, L. (2017). SimplyE—More people discovering more from the library. *D-Lib Magazine, 23*(5/6). https://doi.org/10.1045/may2017-english

Etschmaier, G. S., Sinn, R. N., & Priem, J. (2020). Negotiating big deals: ACRL/SPARC Forum at the 2020 ALA Midwinter Meeting. *College & Research Libraries News, 81*(7). https://doi.org/10.5860/crln.81.7.341

Farley, A., Langham-Putrow, A., Shook, E., Sterman, L. B., & Wacha, M. (2021). Transformative agreements: Six myths, busted. *College & Research Libraries News, 82*(7), 298-301.

Finnie, E. (2016, March 23). What organic food shopping can tell us about transforming the scholarly communications system. *IO: In The Open.* https://web.archive.org/web /20180711230349/http://intheopen.net/2016/03/what-organic-food-shopping-can -tell-us-about-transforming-the-scholarly-communications-system/

FOLIO. (2018, February 9). FOLIO platform begins 2018 with a strong list of accomplishments and plans for rapid expansion over the next twelve months. *FOLIO.* https://www.folio.org/blog/folio-platform-begins-2018-with-a-strong-list-of-ac complishments-and-plans-for-rapid-expansion-over-the-next-twelve-months

Frazier, K. (2001). The librarians' dilemma: Contemplating the costs of the "Big Deal." *D-Lib Magazine, 7*(3). http://www.dlib.org/dlib/march01/frazier/03frazier.html

Goben, A. (2017, December 3). For vs. with: Approaches to librarianship. *Hedgehog Librarian.* http://hedgehoglibrarian.com/2017/12/03/for-vs-with/

Gremmels, G. S. (2013). Staffing trends in college and university libraries. *Reference Services Review, 41*(2), 233–252. https://doi.org/10.1108/00907321311326165

Kennedy, M. R., & LaGuardia, C. (2018). *Marketing your library's electronic resources: A how-to-do-it manual for librarian* (2nd ed.). ALA Neal-Schuman.

Lencioni, P. (2002). *The five dysfunctions of a team: A leadership fable.* Jossey-Bass.

Machovec, G. (2019). Strategies for transformational publish and read agreements in North America. *Journal of Library Administration, 59*(5), 548–555. https://doi.org/10.1080/01930826.2019.1616969

Maddox Abbott, J. A., & Laskowski, M. S. (2014). So many projects, so few resources: Using effective project management in technical services. *Collection Management, 39*(2–3), 161–176. https://doi.org/10.1080/01462679.2014.891492

Maranville, A., & Diaz, K. (2021). The death of the Big Deal and implications for technical services. In S. S. Hines (Ed.), *Technical services in the 21st century* (Vol. 42, pp. 193–212). Emerald Publishing. https://doi.org/10.1108/S0732-06712021 0000042014

Mortimore, J., & Skinner, D. (2017). Shaping expectations: Defining and refining the role of technical services in new resource rollouts. *The Serials Librarian, 72*(1–4), 166–171. https://doi.org/10.1080/0361526X.2017.1285127

Murray, T. E. (2017). An unlikely collaboration: How academic and special libraries can help each other survive. *Journal of Library Administration, 57*(2), 249–258. https://doi.org/10.1080/01930826.2017.1281667

NASIG. (2013). NASIG core competencies for e-resources librarians. https://www.nasig.org/Competencies-Eresources

Neuer, J. (2016, July 21). Introducing SimplyE: 300,000 E-Books to Browse, Borrow, and Read. The New York Public Library. https://www.nypl.org/blog/2016/07/21/introducing-simplye

O'Gara, G., Duncan, C., Lener, E., Blanton-Kent, B., Osterman, A., Durrant, S., Armstrong, A., Donovan, G., & Remhof, T. (2019). Flipping the model: A values-based consortial approach to journal negotiations. *Proceedings of the Charleston Library Conference*, 169–173. https://doi.org/10.5703/1288284317034

O'Gara, G., & Osterman, A. C. (2019). Negotiating on our terms: Harnessing the collective power of the consortium to transform the journal subscription model. *Collection Management, 44*(2–4), 176–194. https://doi.org/10.1080/01462679.2018.1564716

Salo, D. (2011, May 6). Respect my praxis. *#alt-academy: Alternative academic careers.* http://mediacommons.org/alt-ac/pieces/respect-my-praxis

Schachter, D. (2004). Managing your library's technology projects. *Information Outlook, 8*(12), 10–12.

Special Libraries Association. (2021). Competitive and decision intelligence certificate. *Special Libraries Association.* https://www.sla.org/learn-2/certificate-programs /competitive-decision-intelligence-certificate/

SPARC. (2021). InclusiveAccess.org – The Facts on inclusive access textbooks. https://www.inclusiveaccess.org

Sutton, S. W., & Sullenger, P. (2017). The development and use of the NASIG core competencies for electronic resources librarians. *Serials Review, 43*(2), 147–152. https:// doi.org/10.1080/00987913.2017.1316633

Swaak, T. (2021, October 11). Do 'inclusive access' textbook programs save students money? A new site urges everyone to read the fine print. *The Chronicle of Higher Education.* https://www.chronicle.com/article/do-inclusive-access-textbook-programs-save-students-money-a-new-site-urges-everyone-to-read-the-fine-print

Thomas, J., & Noble, M. (2016). The Douglas County model in Western Colorado. *Journal of Library Administration, 56*(3), 326–334. https://doi.org/10.1080/01930826 .2016.1146538

Verminski, A., & Blanchat, K. M. (2017). *Fundamentals of electronic resources management.* ALA Neal-Schuman.

Vinopal, J. (2012). Project portfolio management for academic libraries: A gentle introduction. *College & Research Libraries, 73*(4), 379–389. https://doi.org/10.5860/crl-277

Eleven

Community and Professional Development, and Further Reading

Galadriel Chilton

Andrew Carnegie said that "a library outranks any other one thing a community can do to benefit its people. It is a never-failing spring in the desert," and it is a community of people who manage a library—a network of library staff and libraries that ensure that access to resources remains. Through formal and informal professional development events and conferences, building your own community of e-resource managers will help you continue to learn, work more efficiently and effectively, solve the unsolvable problems, and provide a terrific source of good cheer and humor.

With the resources below, I have included active links as of this writing. Should the links no longer work at the time of your reading, I hope that the names and descriptions of the resource will provide clues and inspiration for seeking out communities of practice and opportunities for professional development.

Additionally, due to the complications that can arise when negotiating, and the necessity for libraries to proactively make certain that commercial resources and their accompanying terms and conditions are appropriate for the users, having a network for discussing approaches and working together when advocacy is needed is paramount. However, please note that some license agreements have legally binding confidentiality clauses. Therefore, proceed cautiously and legally when discussing specifics.

COMMUNITY AND PROFESSIONAL DEVELOPMENT

Following are online discussion lists, online forums, continuing education opportunities, and so on that support e-resources management. Rather than an exhaustive list of possibilities, this is a biased list of my go-to, and most used, resources when I managed e-resources.

Discussion Lists and Forums

Liblicense-L

The discussion list of the Liblicense project (http://liblicense.crl.edu/): "The Liblicense project was created in January 1997, comprising two parts. The Liblicense website provides resources (including model license language and detailed discussion of licensing terms) through an extensive series of links and menus. Liblicense-L is a continuing discussion forum for licensing issues and related contemporary concerns in the domain of scholarly communication. We hope that these materials will serve as a useful starting point toward providing librarians [and staff] with a better understanding of the issues raised by license agreements in the digital age."

ERIL-L

A large, international list, "ERIL's purpose is to provide a forum for discussion of the practical aspects of handling electronic resources and for sharing experiences among ER librarians in this important, developing area of the profession. ERIL subscribers include staff from reference, instruction, technical services, systems, vendors, publishers, and other areas. Examples of issues covered include, but are not limited to, collection development policy, electronic journal holdings, usage statistics, licensing, product setup and maintenance, ERMS development, instruction, and specific product issues, job announcements, news items, and general announcements. Commercial advertisements should not be distributed on ERIL-L. The ERIL list is supported by Electronic Resources & Libraries (http://www.electroniclibrarian.com)."

SERIALST

"SERIALST (Serials in Libraries Discussion Forum) was established in October 1990 by Birdie MacLennan, with technical support from the Office of Academic Computing at the University of Vermont (UVM), in order to serve as an informal electronic forum for most aspects of serials processing in libraries. In 2014, SERIALST moved to NASIG and is now under the management of the Communications & Marketing Committee (CMC). SERIALST's subscriber base is currently at 3,200+ subscribers in 42 countries." (https://www.nasig.org/SERIALST)

LIS-E-RESOURCES

"Email discussion lists for the UK education and research communities." (https://www.jiscmail.ac.uk/cgi-bin/webadmin?A0=LIS-E-RE-SOURCES)

Library Society of the World (LSW)

An informal group of library professionals from all areas of library work and all kinds of libraries. An excellent community for learning, support, and for sharing your questions to get good, thoughtful, and humorous feedback. (https://mokum.place/lsw)

Product-Specific Discussion Lists

For example:

- Your ILS (e.g., Alma or WorldShare)
- EZProxy

Broader Discussion Lists that Include E-Resources and More

For example, lists focusing on topics such as:

- Acquisitions
- Collection development
- Scholarly communication

Professional Development: E-Resource Expert Video Interviews

Sarah Sutton, Assistant Professor of Library and Information Management at Emporia State University, interviewed experts in e-resources management for a course she taught in 2019 as "an open, freely available alternative to requiring the students to purchase a textbook." She completed this project with support of a grant from the Emporia State University Educational Technology Department. https://video.emporia.edu /channel/E-Resources%2BExpert%2BVideo%2BInterviews/123496311

Professional Development: National Conferences in the U.S.

Note: Be sure to check conference websites for scholarships for those new to the field, first-time attendees, and so on. In addition to national conferences, explore state library associations and/or regional chapters of national organizations such as ACRL (Association of College & Research Libraries) for divisions and special interest groups focused on e-resources management.

- CORE (a division of the American Library Association): https:// www.ala.org/core/
- Charleston Conference: Issues in Book and Serial Acquisitions: https://charlestonlibraryconference.com/
- ER&L: http://www.electroniclibrarian.com
- NASIG: http://www.nasig.org/

Continuing Education: Library- and Information Science–Specific

- CORE's continuing education page (https://www.ala.org/core/continuing-education) includes links to past webinars offered by the three ALA divisions that came together to create CORE: ALCTS, LITA, and LLAMA. The Fundamentals web courses (https://www.ala.org/alcts/confevents/upcoming/webcourse) include topics pertinent to e-resources management.
- Institute for Research Design in Librarianship: http://irdlonline.org/
- LYRASIS Learning (https://www.lyrasis.org/Leadership/Pages/LYRASIS-Learning.aspx) offers a variety of classes and courses including copyright, project management, open access, online resource accessibility, etc.
- The Liblicense Project: http://liblicense.crl.edu/ Focusing solely on licensing electronic content, the Liblicense Project's website and companion discussion list offer a wealth of information, sample licensing language, model licenses, etc.

Resources for Open Access and Open Sharing of Research

- ESAC (Efficiency and Standards for Article Charges): https://esac-initiative.org/. Coordinated by the Max Plank Digital Library (https://www.mpdl.mpg.de/en/), EASC is "an open community of information professionals dedicated to putting the vision of open access to research into practice." Their site includes a registry of transformative agreements, recommended workflows, sample agreement terms, and data analytics.
- SPARC (Scholarly Publishing and Academic Resources Coalition) has a Negotiation Community of Practice that developed several resources for libraries and consortia such as data to prepare for Big Deal negotiations (https://sparcopen.org/our-work/negotiation-resources/data-analysis/), and a Big Deal Knowledge Base (https://sparcopen.org/

our-work/big-deal-knowledge-base/). SPARC also provides resources and information about Open Education and Open Data.

Continuing Education: Classes on Specific Skills

Negotiation

- Negotiation Skills for Librarians, by Sarah Durrant of *Lead From Within*
  (http://www.sarahdurrant.co.uk/negotiation-skills-
  for-librarians-online/)
- Harvard Law School's executive education program on negotiation
  (https://www.pon.harvard.edu/executive-education/)

Project Management, Microsoft Excel, and Microsoft Access

- LinkedIn Learning for courses on:
  - Agile project management
  - Microsoft Excel
  - Relational databases in Microsoft Access
- Google/YouTube for quick Excel tips and tricks

FURTHER READING

Following are just a select few of the many books and journals on
e-resources management. These are in addition to the works cited at the
end of each chapter in this book.

Select Publications

Albitz, B. (2008). *Licensing and managing electronic resources.* Chandos.
Ashmore, B., Grogg, J. E., & Weddle, J. (2012). *The librarian's guide to negotiation: Winning
     strategies for the digital age.* Information Today.
Emery, J., Stone, G., & McCracken, P. (2020). *Techniques for electronic resource manage-
     ment: TERMS and the transition to open.* American Library Association.
     https://doi.org/10.15760/lib-01
Johnson, S., Evensen, O. G., Gelfand, J., Lammers, G., Sipe, L., & Zilper, N. (2012).
     Key issues for e-resource collection development: A guide for libraries. IFLA Acquisition

and Collection Development Section. https://www.ifla.org/files/assets/acquisition
-collection-development/publications/electronic-resource-guide-en.pdf

A Few Journals

Journal of Electronic Resources Librarianship https://www.tandfonline.com/toc
/wacq20/current
Journal of Librarianship & Scholarly Communication https://jlsc-pub.org/
Weave: Journal of Library User Experience https://www.weaveux.org/about.html

Epilogue

Galadriel Chilton

As every theatrical performance or movie production has its accompanying, and often never-told, stories from behind the scenes, so too does this book have the story of how it came to be.

While it's not as amusing as a blooper reel, given the topics covered in this book—especially Chapter 4 on licensing—it's a story to be shared. However, because I am not a lawyer nor do I retain legal counsel, certain details will be anonymized or omitted.

After a publisher accepted the proposal for this book, I received the author agreement. Just as I would review a license agreement for e-resources, I reviewed the agreement. Then, I returned a redlined agreement noting requested changes I had using Microsoft Word's track changes.

My biggest concern with the publisher's agreement was the presence of an indemnification clause whereby "the Authors/Editors shall indemnify and hold [Publisher] harmless against loss of expenses arising from breach of any such warranties." Many academic libraries—per their organization's legal counsel—seek to strike indemnification clauses in e-resource agreements.

Additionally, I as an individual have neither a desire to, nor am I in a financial position to, pay lawyer fees, court costs, or damage awards for any claims as agreeing to the indemnity clause would require, should any claims arise.

My expectation is that publishers, with their experience and legal counsel, have a much better grasp of the risks associated with any given publication, and thus should a) accept such risks as part of doing business, and b) communicate any such risks to authors as part of the publication process, so that risks can be avoided. (I realize that this expectation is idealistic, but it's there nonetheless.)

In due course, the publisher sent a new author agreement, one that reflected all the changes I had requested, including the removal of the indemnification clause.

I signed the agreement and began working on the text.

With the passage of time, I realized that this text would be significantly better if it included the voices of more colleagues who could write to their experiences suddenly managing e-resources, and so, this project evolved.

Given this change, I alerted the editor, who noted that they had contacted the publisher about sending each of the new contributors an author agreement. While waiting for the author agreement to be sent to them, the contributors all began working on the text in good faith, because I, in good faith given the agreement I had signed, had asked them to. This was a very regrettable mistake on my part.

When the publisher sent the author agreement to contributors several months later, the agreement contained an indemnification clause. One of the contributors removed the clause before signing and returning it to the publisher. The publisher declined, and I asked the publisher to remove the clause, pointing out that my signed agreement excluded this clause, and that colleagues worked for institutions that could not sign agreements with indemnity clauses; therefore, I could not expect them to agree.

The publisher declined, noting that it could not remove the indemnity clause for copyright and legal reasons and that if the contributors could not accept the indemnity clause, I would need to find new contributors.

I again pointed out that there was precedent for the publisher removing the clause, given that it was not in my agreement. Additionally, I could not in good conscience ask contributors to accept contract language for an author agreement that they work to have removed from their institution's e-resource licenses, and that in this work's text the authors recommend it be removed from license agreements.

This is when, quite unexpectedly, the publisher noted that it was sorry I was under the impression that the agreement I had signed had been accepted, because since the agreement had not been countersigned, it was not fully executed and still under review. I had never been told that agreement was under review, and thus I had begun working on the text. If further review and revision was needed with the signed agreement, I would have expected the publisher to notify the authors immediately. This was also a mistake and a case of misplaced optimism and expectations on my part.

After several e-mail exchanges, including ones where I forwarded the messages to the publisher documenting where it had asked us to sign the new agreement with the associated attachment that excluded an indemnification clause, I received a message of apology noting that this agreement—the one I had signed without the indemnification clause—was sent to us "erroneously" and that because the contributors cannot agree to the indemnification clause, the publisher will not continue to work on this project. The publisher noted that it could not afford to respond to any legal ramifications if a publication violated one of its warranties.

That this publisher expects authors to agree to terms and conditions that library staff on behalf of their libraries cannot agree to when negotiating license agreements, and that the Authors Guild recommends negotiating these terms out of author agreements (or at least modifying), is unfortunate (https://www.authorsguild.org/wp-content/uploads/2016/01/AG-FCI_Eight-Principles_final-1.pdf).

Thus, this text now reaches you via Pacific University Press! I am incredibly grateful to Isaac Gilman and the editorial board for working with us to fulfill my goal of this project: for colleagues new to e-resources management to have access to concrete information to help them succeed

in their work, and for students in library and information science programs to have access (without charge, through the authors' institutional
repositories and other open-access venues) to a text that would help
them understand—and potentially pursue—this complex, ever-evolving,
and critical part of library work.

So, to conclude this text on managing e-resources, I leave you with
these lessons I learned:

- Always carefully read and negotiate author agreements, just as you
  would always carefully read and negotiate e-resource license agreements, and know that the publishers you would think would have the
  best author agreements for you as an author are the ones that may sur-
  prise you the most.
- Get a countersigned, fully executed author agreement before
  proceeding.
- If a publisher will not accept the changes you've requested, seek a different publisher. I've worked with publishers that a) didn't have an
  indemnification clause in the agreement to begin with, b) removed it
  upon my request without question, or c) accepted modified indemnification language.

Author Bios

Galadriel Chilton

Director of Collections Initiatives for the Ivy Plus Libraries Confederation, a partnership of 13 academic libraries. In this role, Galadriel plans, implements, and oversees collaborative collection initiatives with her colleagues. She has taught e-resources management and licensing classes for the University of Wisconsin iSchool and guided a new e-resources management team into a high-functioning group. At the 2014 Electronic Resources & Libraries Conference, her presentation, *Human TERMS of Engagement*, focused on the need for more library staff to have the skills and knowledge needed to manage e-resources, which was an early inkling for this book. She has a BA in English from Berea College, a Master of Library Science from Indiana University, a Master of Education in Instructional Design and Educational Technology from San Diego State University, and a certificate in project management from Cornell University.

Stephanie Willen Brown

Director of the Park Library at the University of North Carolina at Chapel Hill's Hussman School of Journalism and Media. Stephanie went to college & graduate school in Massachusetts (A.B., Mount Holyoke College and M.S. from Simmons' Graduate School of Library and Information Science) in the last century, and started working at UNC in 2009. She loves cats, her spouse, and photography. Her favorite work thing is talking to students about finding useful resources for their projects. She is able to easily switch between doing broad Google searches and targeted, highly relevant library database searches. She teaches reference at UNC's School of Information and Library Science.

Anna Creech

Head of Resource Acquisition and Delivery, Boatwright Memorial Library, University of Richmond. Anna has worked with serials and electronic resources throughout her career, from cataloging to licensing and assessment. She has used different electronic resource management (ERM) tools and catalog systems to do these things, as well as far too many spreadsheets than any one person should have to work with. In recent years, her responsibilities have shifted to include library collection development as a whole.

Lindsay Cronk

Head of Collection Strategies and Scholarly Communications at the University of Rochester. Lindsay has worked in a variety of leadership positions in consortia and academic libraries. While completing her MLIS, she worked at LYRASIS, where she gained a broader view of the scholarly communication landscape and the importance of strategic partnerships between libraries and vendors. Working in academic libraries, she has translated this experience into her development and deployment of collection assessment and strategy. She prides herself on her Midwestern friendliness and sledgehammer directness.

Joan M. Emmet

Licensing and Copyright Librarian, Yale University (retired). Joan chaired the License Review Team who reviewed all licenses prior to the purchase or lease of e-resources. She consulted with students, faculty and staff about copyright issues and author agreements. She worked closely with the Yale Office of General Counsel in review of a variety of library contracts for services. Prior to Joan's position as Licensing and Copyright Librarian, she was director of the NERL Consortium and responsible for consortial licensing of e-resources and e-resource pricing negotiations. Joan has presented on the topic of licensing and copyright at numerous workshops and seminars. In addition, Joan has created and hosted programs for Open Access Week and Fair Use Week at Yale. Joan is presently enjoying retirement by playing guitar, throwing pots, keeping abreast of copyright, estates, and probate issues, and enjoys catching up with former colleagues.

Scarlet Galvan

Collection Strategist Librarian, Grand Valley State University. Scarlet Galvan is the Area Lead for Assessment and Planning, and Collection Strategist Librarian at Grand Valley State University Libraries. At GVSU she develops and leads efforts toward a more sustainable, open collection. Her research focuses on the sociopolitical aspects of library services platforms and scholarly communications. When not negotiating resources for the library, she writes science fiction and makes soap.

Athena Hoeppner

Discovery Services Librarian, University of Central Florida Libraries.

Jenifer S. Holman

Electronic Resources Librarian, Hope College.

Allyson Rodriguez

Assistant Director of Library Services, Jenkins Garrett Library, Tarrant County College.

Erika Ripley

Head, Resource Acquisitions & Management, University of North Carolina Libraries. Erika Ripley is the Head of Resource Acquisitions & Management at The University of North Carolina, University Libraries. In this role, she leads the team responsible for materials acquisitions in all formats including the licensing and management of e-resources. It is her belief that this work, no matter where it is situated organizationally, is best done when it is considered public services work.

Angela Sidman

Director of E-Resources and Serials Management, Yale University Library.

Acknowledgments

Galadriel is incredibly grateful to:

- The contributors to this book for joining me on this book-writing adventure and for making it far better than I ever envisioned. Stephanie, Anna, Lyndsay, Joan, Scarlet, Athena, Jen, Erika, Allyson, and Angela: Thank you for being such incredible colleagues and collaborators.
- The anonymous peer reviewers, for your time and thoughtful feedback—thank you.
- Hillary Corbett for her superb copyediting, and Alex Bell for designing a book cover that so aptly represents the text.
- Isaac Gilman, Dean of University Libraries at Pacific University Libraries, and members of the editorial board at Pacific University Press, for giving this book a home.
- Gerard and Cian Ferrari, for their presence and support; thank you and love you always!

Index

*Note: The Glossary of Terms (Chapter 2) includes definitions of index terms in **bold**.*

CPSIA information can be obtained
at www.ICGtesting.com
Printed in the USA
JSHW061750290722
28601JS00003B/165